Cisco Networking Academy Program
CCNA 3 and 4 Lab Companion
Third Edition

Cisco Systems, Inc.
Cisco Networking Academy Program

Cisco Press

800 East 96th Street
Indianapolis, IN 46240 USA

Cisco Networking Academy Program
CCNA 3 and 4 Lab Companion
Third Edition

Cisco Systems, Inc.
Cisco Networking Academy Program

Copyright © 2003 Cisco Systems, Inc.

Published by:
Cisco Press
800 East 96th Street
Indianapolis, IN 46240 USA

Printed in the United States of America   3 4 5 6 7 8 9 0

Third Printing September 2004

ISBN: 1-58713-114-5

Warning and Disclaimer

This book is designed to provide information on *CCNA 3: Switching Basics and Intermediate Routing* and *CCNA 4: WAN Technologies* of the Cisco Networking Academy Program CCNA course. Every effort has been made to make this book as complete and as accurate as possible, but no warranty or fitness is implied.

The information is provided on an "as is" basis. The author, Cisco Press, and Cisco Systems, Inc. shall have neither liability nor responsibility to any person or entity with respect to any loss or damages arising from the information contained in this book or from the use of the programs that may accompany it.

The opinions expressed in this book belong to the author and are not necessarily those of Cisco Systems, Inc.

CISCO SYSTEMS

This book is part of the Cisco Networking Academy® Program series from Cisco Press. The products in this series support and complement the Cisco Networking Academy Program curriculum. If you are using this book outside the Networking Academy program, then you are not preparing with a Cisco trained and authorized Networking Academy provider.

For information on the Cisco Networking Academy Program or to locate a Networking Academy, please visit www.cisco.com/edu.

Trademark Acknowledgments

All terms mentioned in this book that are known to be trademarks or service marks have been appropriately capitalized. Cisco Press or Cisco Systems, Inc., cannot attest to the accuracy of this information. Use of a term in this book should not be regarded as affecting the validity of any trademark or service mark.

Corporate and Government Sales

Cisco Press offers excellent discounts on this book when ordered in quantity for bulk purchases or special sales.

For more information please contact: **U.S. Corporate and Government Sales** 1-800-382-3419
corpsales@pearsontechgroup.com

For sales outside the U.S. please contact: **International Sales** international@pearsoned.com

Feedback Information

At Cisco Press, our goal is to create in-depth technical books of the highest quality and value. Each book is crafted with care and precision, undergoing rigorous development that involves the unique expertise of members of the professional technical community.

Readers' feedback is a natural continuation of this process. If you have any comments regarding how we could improve the quality of this book or otherwise alter it to better suit your needs, you can contact us at networkingacademy@ciscopress.com. Please be sure to include the book title and ISBN in your message.

We greatly appreciate your assistance.

Publisher	John Wait
Editor-in-Chief	John Kane
Executive Editor	Mary Beth Ray
Cisco Systems Representative	Anthony Wolfenden
Cisco Press Program Manager	Nannette M. Noble
Production Manager	Patrick Kanouse
Development Editor	Christopher Cleveland
Technical Editors	Jim Lorenz
	Clifton Croom
Copy Editor	Karen A. Gill

Corporate Headquarters
Cisco Systems, Inc.
170 West Tasman Drive
San Jose, CA 95134-1706
USA
www.cisco.com
Tel: 408 526-4000
    800 553-NETS (6387)
Fax: 408 526-4100

European Headquarters
Cisco Systems International BV
Haarlerbergpark
Haarlerbergweg 13-19
1101 CH Amsterdam
The Netherlands
www-europe.cisco.com
Tel: 31 0 20 357 1000
Fax: 31 0 20 357 1100

Americas Headquarters
Cisco Systems, Inc.
170 West Tasman Drive
San Jose, CA 95134-1706
USA
www.cisco.com
Tel: 408 526-7660
Fax: 408 527-0883

Asia Pacific Headquarters
Cisco Systems, Inc.
Capital Tower
168 Robinson Road
#22-01 to #29-01
Singapore 068912
www.cisco.com
Tel: +65 6317 7777
Fax: +65 6317 7799

Cisco Systems has more than 200 offices in the following countries and regions. Addresses, phone numbers, and fax numbers are listed on the
Cisco.com Web site at www.cisco.com/go/offices.

Argentina • Australia • Austria • Belgium • Brazil • Bulgaria • Canada • Chile • China PRC • Colombia • Costa Rica • Croatia • Czech Republic
Denmark • Dubai, UAE • Finland • France • Germany • Greece • Hong Kong SAR • Hungary • India • Indonesia • Ireland • Israel • Italy
Japan • Korea • Luxembourg • Malaysia • Mexico • The Netherlands • New Zealand • Norway • Peru • Philippines • Poland • Portugal
Puerto Rico • Romania • Russia • Saudi Arabia • Scotland • Singapore • Slovakia • Slovenia • South Africa • Spain • Sweden
Switzerland • Taiwan • Thailand • Turkey • Ukraine • United Kingdom • United States • Venezuela • Vietnam • Zimbabwe

Table of Contents

Foreword

Throughout the world, the Internet has brought tremendous new opportunities for individuals and their employers. Companies and other organizations are seeing dramatic increases in productivity by investing in robust networking capabilities. Some studies have shown measurable productivity improvements in entire economies. The promise of enhanced efficiency, profitability, and standard of living is real and growing.

Such productivity gains aren't achieved by simply purchasing networking equipment. Skilled professionals are needed to plan, design, install, deploy, configure, operate, maintain, and troubleshoot today's networks. Network managers need to assure that they've planned for network security and for continued operation. They need to design for the performance level required in their organization. They need to implement new capabilities as the demands of their organization, and its reliance on the network, expands.

To meet the many educational needs of the internetworking community, Cisco established the Cisco Networking Academy Program. The Cisco Networking Academy Program is a comprehensive learning program that provides students with the Internet technology skills essential in a global economy. The Networking Academy program integrates face-to-face teaching, web-based content, online assessment, student performance tracking, hands-on labs, instructor training and support, and preparation for industry-standard certifications.

The Networking Academy program continually raises the bar on blended learning and educational processes. The Internet-based assessment and instructor support systems are some of the most extensive and validated ever developed, including a 24/7 customer service system for Academy instructors. Through community feedback and electronic assessment, the Networking Academy program adapts curriculum to improve outcomes and student achievement. The Cisco Global Learning Network infrastructure designed for the Networking Academy program delivers a rich, interactive, and personalized curriculum to students around the world. The Internet has the power to change the way people work, live, play and learn, and the Cisco Networking Academy Program is in the forefront of this transformation.

This Cisco Press title is one of a series of best-selling companion titles for the Cisco Networking Academy Program. These books are designed by Cisco Worldwide Education and Cisco Press to provide integrated support for the online learning content that is made available to Academies all over the world. These Cisco Press books are the only books authorized for the Academy program by Cisco Systems, and provide print and CD-ROM materials that help ensure the greatest possible learning experience for Networking Academy students.

I hope you are successful as you embark on your learning path with Cisco and the Internet. I also hope that you'll choose to continue your learning after you complete the Academy curriculum. In addition to its Cisco Networking Academy titles, Cisco Press also publishes an extensive list of networking technology and certification publications that provide a wide range of resources. Cisco has also established a network of professional training companies—the Cisco Learning Partners—who provide a full range of Cisco training courses. They offer training in many formats, including e-learning, self-paced, and instructor-led classes. Their instructors are certified by Cisco, and their materials are created by Cisco. When you're ready, please visit the Learning & Events area on www.cisco.com to learn about all the educational support that Cisco and its partners have to offer.

Thank you for choosing this book and the Cisco Networking Academy Program.

Kevin Warner

Senior Director, Marketing

Worldwide Education

Cisco Systems, Inc.

Introduction

The *Cisco Networking Academy Program CCNA 3 and 4 Lab Companion* supplements version 3.x of the online course and the companion guide. It provides hands-on experience along with review questions to support the material covered. This book is useful in its own right as a network configuration basics lab manual.

The topics that are covered in the book introduce and extend your knowledge and practical experience with the design, configuration, and maintenance of switches, LANs, and virtual local-area networks (VLANs).

This book contains all of the labs in version 3.x of the CCNA 3 and CCNA 4 curriculum of the Cisco Networking Academy Program. Most of the labs are hands on and require access to a Cisco Router Lab or a Simulator.

Who Should Read This Book

The book is written for anyone who wants to learn about networking technologies. Students in high schools, community colleges, and four-year institutions are the main target audience for this book. Specifically, in an educational environment, this book can be used in the classroom as a lab manual.

This Book's Organization

Table I-1 outlines all the labs in this book, the corresponding Target Indicator (TI) used in the online curriculum, the time it should take to do the lab, and the difficulty rating (1 to 3, with 3 being the most difficult).

Table I-1   Master Lab Overview

Lab Number	Title	TI	Difficulty	Estimated Time
CCNA 3 Labs				
Lab 2-1	Calculating VLSM Subnets	1.1.4	3	30
Lab 2-2	Review of Basic Router Configuration with RIP	1.2.3	2	20
Lab 2-3	Converting RIP Version 1 to RIP Version 2	1.2.4	2	15
Lab 2-4	Verifying RIP Version 2 Configuration	1.2.5	2	20
Lab 2-5	Troubleshooting RIP Version 2 by Using **debug**	1.2.6	2	20

Lab Number	Title	TI	Difficulty	Estimated Time
Lab 3-1	Configuring the OSPF Routing Process	2.3.1	2	20
Lab 3-2	Configuring OSPF with Loopback Addresses	2.3.2	2	20
Lab 3-3	Modifying OSPF Cost Metric	2.3.3	2	20
Lab 3-4	Configuring OSPF Authentication	2.3.4	2	15
Lab 3-5	Configuring OSPF Timers	2.3.5	2	15
Lab 3-6	Propagating Default Routes in an OSPF Domain	2.3.6	2	15
Lab 4-1	Configuring EIGRP Routing	3.2.1	2	20
Lab 4-2	Verifying Basic EIGRP Configuration	3.2.3	2	20
Lab 7-1	Verifying Default Switch Configuration	6.2.1	1	15
Lab 7-2	Basic Switch Configuration	6.2.2	2	20
Lab 7-3	Managing the MAC Address Table	6.2.3	2	15
Lab 7-4	Configuring Static MAC Addresses	6.2.4	2	15
Lab 7-5	Configuring Port Security	6.2.5	2	15
Lab 7-6	Add, Move, and Change MAC Addresses	6.2.6	2	15
Lab 7-7	Managing Switch Operating System Images	6.2.7a	2	30
Lab 7-8	Managing Switch Startup Configuration Files	6.2.7b	2	30

Lab Number	Title	TI	Difficulty	Estimated Time
Lab 7-9	Password Recovery Procedure for a Catalyst 2900 Series Switch	6.2.8	2	30
Lab 7-10	Firmware Upgrade of a Catalyst 2900 Series Switch	6.2.9	2	30
Lab 8-1	Selecting the Root Bridge	7.2.4	2	30
Lab 8-2	Spanning Tree Recalculation	7.2.6	2	30
Lab 9-1	Configuring Static VLANs	8.2.3	2	30
Lab 9-2	Verifying VLAN Configurations	8.2.4	2	30
Lab 9-3	Deleting VLAN Configurations	8.2.6	2	30
Lab 10-1	Trunking with ISL	9.1.5a	2	30
Lab 10-2	Trunking with 802.1q	9.1.5b	2	30
Lab 10-3	VTP Client and Server Configuration	9.2.5	2	30
Lab 10-4	Configuring Inter-VLAN Routing	9.3.6	3	30
CCNA 4 Labs				
Lab 11-1	Configuring NAT	1.1.4a	3	20
Lab 11-2	Configuring PAT	1.1.4b	3	20
Lab 11-3	Configuring Static NAT Addresses	1.1.4c	3	20
Lab 11-4	Verifying NAT and PAT Configuration	1.1.5	3	20
Lab 11-5	Troubleshooting NAT and PAT	1.1.6	3	20
Lab 11-6	Configuring DHCP	1.2.6	3	20
Lab 11-7	Configuring DHCP Relay	1.2.8	3	20

Lab Number	Title	TI	Difficulty	Estimated Time
Lab 13-1	Troubleshooting a Serial Interface	3.1.7	2	15
Lab 13-2	Configuring PPP Encapsulation	3.3.2	2	15
Lab 13-3	Configuring PPP Authentication	3.3.3	3	20
Lab 13-4	Verifying the PPP Configuration	3.3.4	2	15
Lab 13-5	Troubleshooting PPP Configuration	3.3.5	2	15
Lab 14-1	Configuring ISDN BRI (U-Interface)	4.2.1	3	30
Lab 14-2	Configuring Legacy DDR	4.3.2	3	30
Lab 14-3	Configuring Dialer Profiles	4.3.7	3	30
Lab 15-1	Configuring Frame Relay	5.2.1	3	30
Lab 15-2	Configuring Frame Relay PVC	5.2.2	3	30
Lab 15-3	Configuring Frame Relay Subinterfaces	5.2.5	3	30

This Book's Features

Many of this book's features facilitate a full understanding of the networking and routing topics that are covered in this book:

Objectives and Scenarios—Each lab in this manual provides an objective, or a goal of the lab. The equipment required is listed and a scenario is provided that allows you to relate the exercise to real-world environments.

Reflection Questions—So that you can demonstrate an understanding of the concepts covered, reflection questions are provided throughout the labs where appropriate. In addition, some questions are included to elicit particular points of understanding. These questions help verify your comprehension of the technology that is being implemented.

The conventions that present command syntax in this book are the same conventions that are used in the Cisco IOS Command Reference:

- Bold indicates commands and keywords that are entered literally as shown. In examples (not syntax), bold indicates user input (such as a show command).

- Italic indicates arguments for which you supply values.

- Braces ({ }) indicate a required element.

- Square brackets ([ ]) indicate an optional element.

- Vertical bars (|) separate alternative, mutually exclusive elements.

- Braces and vertical bars within square brackets (such as [x {y | z}]) indicate a required choice within an optional element. You do not need to enter what is in the brackets, but if you do, you have some required choices in the braces.

Part I   CCNA 3: Switching Basics and Intermediate Routing

CCNA 3

Chapter 1: Review: The OSI Reference Model and Routing

There are no hands-on labs associated with the topic of this chapter. Please review the information in Chapter 1 of the *Cisco Networking Academy Program CCNA 3 and 4 Companion Guide* to ensure that you can do the following:

- Describe the OSI reference model's overall function and the problems it solves
- Describe the characteristics of the OSI reference model's physical layer
- Describe the characteristics of the OSI reference model's data link layer
- Describe the characteristics of the OSI reference model's network layer
- Describe the characteristics of the OSI reference model's transport layer
- Describe the function of routing in networks
- Understand the different classes of routing protocols

CCNA 3

Chapter 2: Introduction to Classless Routing

The following table maps the numbering scheme used in this chapter's labs to the Target Indicators (TIs) used in the online curriculum.

Lab Companion Numbering	Online Curriculum TI
Lab 2-1	1.1.4
Lab 2-2	1.2.3
Lab 2-3	1.2.4
Lab 2-4	1.2.5
Lab 2-5	1.2.6

Lab 2-1   Calculating VLSM Subnets (TI 1.1.4)

Figure 2-1.1 Topology for Lab 2-1

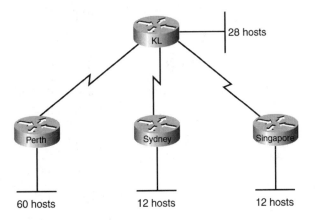

Objective

Use variable-length subnet mask (VLSM) to support more efficient use of the assigned IP address and to reduce the amount of routing information at the top level.

Background/Preparation

A Class C address of 192.168.10.0/24 has been allocated.

Perth, Sydney, and Singapore have a WAN connection to Kuala Lumpur.

- Perth requires 60 hosts.
- Kuala Lumpur requires 28 hosts.
- Sydney and Singapore each require 12 hosts.

To calculate VLSM subnets and the respective hosts, allocate the largest requirements first from the address range. Requirements levels should be listed from the largest to the smallest.

In this example, Perth requires 60 hosts. Use 6 bits because $2^6 - 2 = 62$ usable host addresses. Thus, 2 bits will be used from the fourth octet to represent the extended network prefix of /26, and the remaining 6 bits will be used for host addresses.

Step 1. Divide the allocated addresses into four equal sized address blocks.

The first step in the subnetting process is to divide the allocated address of 192.168.10.0/24 into four equal sized address blocks. Because $4 = 2^2$, 2 bits are required to identify each of the 4 subnets.

Next, take subnet #0 (192.168.10.0/26) and identify each of its hosts. Table 2-1.1 documents the allocated addresses, subnetworks, and usable hosts.

Table 2-1.1   Usable Hosts for 192.168.10.0/24

Allocated Address	Subnetworks	62 Usable Hosts/Subnetworks (Subnet #0)
192.168.10.0/24	192.168.10.0/26	192.168.10.0/26 (network address)
	192.168.10.64/26	192.168.10.1/26
	192.168.10.128/26	192.168.10.2/26
	192.168.10.192/26	192.168.10.3/26
		through
		192.168.10.61/26
		192.168.10.62/26
		192.168.10.63/26 (broadcast address)

Table 2-1.2 lists the range for the /26 mask.

Table 2-1.2   IP Address Range for 192.168.10.0/26

Perth	Range of Addresses in the Last Octet
192.168.10.0/26	From 0 to 63. 60 hosts required.
	Hosts 0 and 63 cannot be used because they are the network and broadcast addresses for their subnet. 62 useable addresses are available for assignment to hosts.

Step 2. Allocate the next level after all the requirements are met for the higher level(s).

Kuala Lumpur requires 28 hosts. The next available address after 192.168.10.63/26 is 192.168.10.64/26. Note from the preceding table that this is subnet#1. Because 28 hosts are required, $2^5 - 2 = 30$ usable network addresses. Thus, 5 bits will be required to represent the hosts, and 3 bits will be used to represent the extended network prefix of /27. Applying VLSM on address 192.168.10.64/27 gives the results in Table 2-1.3.

Table 2-1.3   Usable Hosts for 192.168.10.64/26

Subnetwork #1	Sub-Subnetworks	30 Usable Hosts (192.168.10.64/27 Subnet)
192.168.10.64/26	192.168.10.64/27	192.168.10.64/27 (network address)
	192.168.10.96/27	192.168.10.65/27
	192.168.10.128/27	192.168.10.66/27
	192.168.10.192/27	192.168.10.67/26
		through
		192.168.10.93/27
		192.168.10.94/27
		192.168.10.95/27 (broadcast address)

Table 2-1.4 lists the range for the /27 mask.

Table 2-1.4   IP Address Range for 192.168.10.64/27

Kuala Lumpur	Range of Addresses in the Last Octet
192.168.10.64/27	From 64 to 95. 28 hosts required. Hosts 64 and 95 cannot be used because they are the network and broadcast addresses for their subnet. 30 usable addresses are available in this range for the hosts.

Step 3. Sydney and Singapore require 12 hosts each. The next available address starts from 192.168.10.96/27. Note from Table 2-1.3 that this is the next subnet available. Because 12 hosts are required, $2^4 - 2 = 14$ usable addresses. Thus, 4 bits are required to represent the hosts, and 4 bits are required for the extended network prefix of /28. Applying VLSM on address 192.168.10.96/27 gives the results in Table 2-1.5.

Table 2-1.5   Usable Hosts for 192.168.10.96/27

Subnetwork	Sub-Subnetworks	14 Usable Hosts (192.168.10.96/28 Subnet)
192.168.10.96/27	192.168.10.96/28	192.168.10.96/28 (network address)
	192.168.10.112/28	192.168.10.97/28
	192.168.10.128/28	192.168.10.98/28
	192.168.10.224/28	192.168.10.99/28
	192.168.10.240/28	through
		192.168.10.109/28
		192.168.10.110/28
		192.168.10.111/28 (broadcast address)

Table 2-1.6 lists the range for the /28 mask.

Table 2-1.6   IP Address Range for 192.168.10.96/28

Sydney	Range of Addresses in the Last Octet
192.168.10.96/28	From 96 to 111. 12 hosts required. Hosts 96 and 111 cannot be used because they are network and broadcast addresses for their subnet. 14 usable addresses are available in this range for the hosts.

Step 4. Because Singapore also requires 12 hosts, the next set of host addresses in Table 2-1.7 can be derived from the next available subnet (192.168.10.112/28).

Table 2-1.7   Singapore Host Addresses

Sub-Subnetworks	14 Usable Hosts (192.168.10.112/28 Subnet)
192.168.10.96/28	**192.168.10.112/28 (network address)**
192.168.10.112/28	192.168.10.113/28
192.168.10.128/28	192.168.10.114/28
192.168.10.224/28	192.168.10.115/28
	through
192.168.10.240/28	192.168.10.125/28
	192.168.10.126/28
	192.168.10.127/28 (broadcast address)

Table 2-1.8 lists the range for the /28 mask.

Table 2-1.8   IP Address Range for 192.168.10.112/28

Singapore	Range of Addresses in the Last Octet
192.168.10.112/28	From 112 to 127. 12 hosts required. Hosts 112 and 127 cannot be used because they are network and broadcast addresses for their subnet. 14 usable addresses are available in this range for the hosts.

Step 5. Now allocate addresses for the WAN links. Remember that each WAN link requires two IP addresses. The next available subnet is 192.168.10.128/28. Because 2 network addresses are required for each WAN link, $2^2 - 2 = 2$ usable addresses. Thus, 2 bits are required to represent the links, and 6 bits are required for the extended network prefix of /30. Applying VLSM on 192.168.10.128/28 gives the results in Table 2-1.9.

Table 2-1.6   Usable Hosts After Applying VLSM on 192.168.10.112/28

Sub-Subnetworks	2 Usable Hosts per Subnet
192.168.10.128/30	192.168.10.128/30 (network address)
	192.168.10.129/30
	192.168.10.130/30
	192.168.10.31/30 (broadcast address)
192.168.10.132/30	192.168.10.132/30 (network address)
	192.168.10.133/30
	192.168.10.134/30
	192.168.10.135/30 (broadcast address)
192.168.10.136/30	192.168.10.136/30 (network address)
	192.168.10.137/30
	192.168.10.138/30
	192.168.10.139/30 (broadcast address)

The addresses for the WAN links can be taken from the available addresses in each of the /30 subnets.

Step 6. Using the lab diagram, document the correct VLSM subnet number to be applied next to each subnetwork and write a valid IP address next to each router interface.

Lab 2-2   Review of Basic Router Configuration with RIP (TI 1.2.3)

Figure 2-2.1 Topology for Lab 2-2

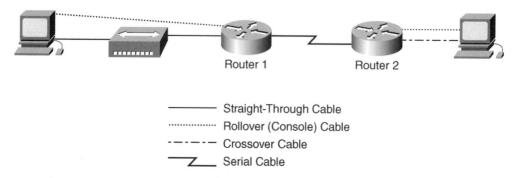

```
—————————      Straight-Through Cable
..............      Rollover (Console) Cable
— — — —      Crossover Cable
  Z          Serial Cable
```

Table 2-2.1   Lab Equipment Configuration

Router Designation	Router Name	Fast Ethernet0 Address	Interface Type	Serial 0 Address
Router 1	GAD	172.16.0.1	DCE	172.17.0.1
Router 2	BHM	172.18.0.1	DTE	172.17.0.2

The enable secret password for both routers is **class**.

The enable, VTY, and console password for both routers is **cisco**.

The subnet mask for both interfaces on both routers is 255.255.0.0.

Objective

- Cable and configure workstations and routers.
- Set up an IP addressing scheme by using Class B networks.
- Configure RIP on routers.

Background/Preparation

Cable a network that is similar to the one in Figure 2-2.1. You can use any router that meets the interface requirements in Figure 2-2.1 (that is, 800, 1600, 1700, 2500, and 2600 routers or a combination). Refer to the information in Appendix C, "Router Interface Summary Chart," to correctly specify the interface identifiers based on the equipment in your lab. The 1721 series routers produced the configuration output in this lab. Another router might produce slightly different output. You should execute the following steps on each router unless you are specifically instructed otherwise. Implement the procedure documented in Appendix A, "Erasing and Reloading the Router," before you continue with this lab.

General Configuration Tips

- Use the question mark (**?**) and arrow keys help to enter commands.

- Each command mode restricts the set of available commands. If you have difficulty entering a command, check the prompt and then enter the question mark (**?**) for a list of available commands. The problem might be a wrong command mode or wrong syntax.

- To disable a feature, enter the keyword **no** before the command; for example, **no ip routing**.

- Save the configuration changes to nonvolatile RAM (NVRAM) so that the changes are not lost if there is a system reload or power outage.

Table 2-2.2 lists the router command modes for this and other labs in the chapter.

Table 2-2.2   Router Command Modes

Command Mode	Access Method	Router Prompt Displayed	Exit Method
User EXEC	Log in.	Router>	Use the **logout** command.
Privileged EXEC	From user EXEC mode, enter the **enable** command.	Router#	To exit to user EXEC mode, use the **disable**, **exit**, or **logout** command.
Global configuration	From the privileged EXEC mode, enter the **configure terminal** command.	Router(config)#	To exit to privileged EXEC mode, use the **exit** or **end** command, or press **Ctrl+Z**.
Interface configuration	From the global configuration mode, enter the **interface** *type number* command, such as **interface serial 0**.	Router(config-if)#	To exit to global configuration mode, use the **exit** command.

Step 1. Basic router configuration.

Connect a rollover cable to the console port on the router and the other end to the PC with a DB9 or DB25 adapter to a COM port. You should do this prior to powering on any devices.

Step 2. Start the HyperTerminal program.

    A.   Turn on the computer and router.

    B.   From the Windows taskbar, locate the HyperTerminal program by clicking **Start**>**Programs**>**Accessories**>**Communications**>**HyperTerminal**.

Step 3. Name the HyperTerminal session.

At the Connection Description popup, enter a name in the connection Name field and select OK (see Figure 2-2.2).

Figure 2-2.2 HyperTerminal Connection Description Dialog Box

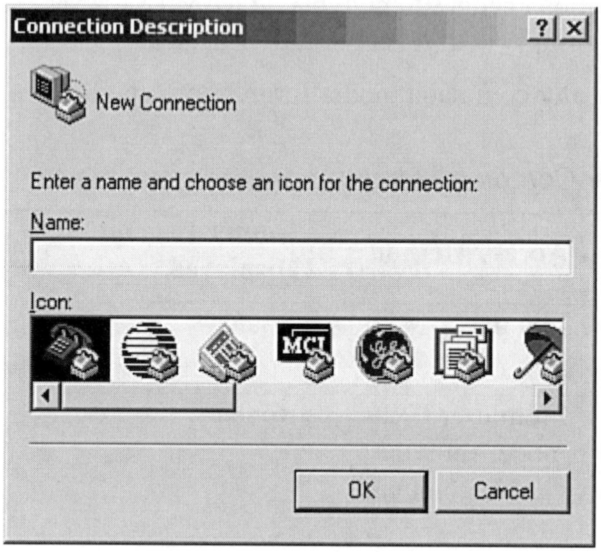

Step 4. Specify the computer's connecting interface.

At the Connect To popup, use the drop-down arrow in the Connect Using field to select **COM1** and select **OK** (see Figure 2-2.3).

Figure 2-2.3 HyperTerminal Connect To Dialog Box

Step 5. Specify the interface connection properties.

A.   At the COM1 Properties popup, use the drop-down arrows to select the following:

Bits per second = **9600**

Data Bits = **8**

Parity = **None**

Stop bits = **1**

Flow control = **None**

Then select **OK** (see Figure 2-2.4).

Figure 2-2.4 HyperTerminal Interface Connection Property Settings

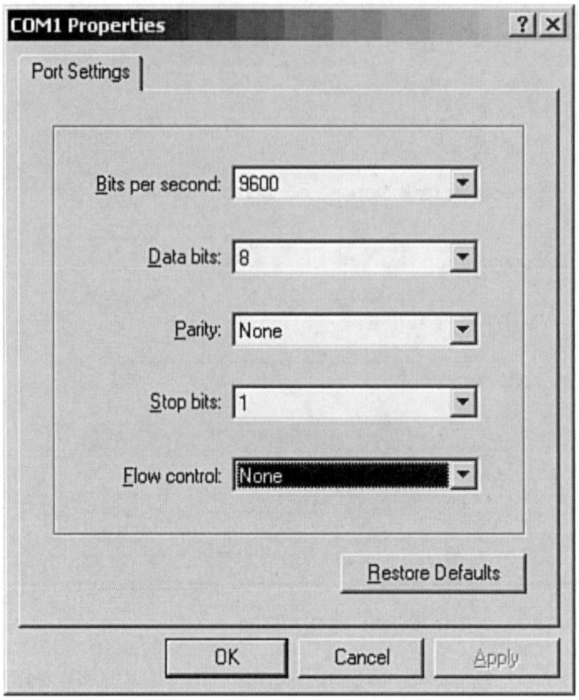

B.   When the HyperTerminal session window comes up (see Figure 2-2.5),
        turn on the router. If the router is already on, press the **Enter** key. The
        router should respond.

Figure 2-2.5 HyperTerminal Session Window

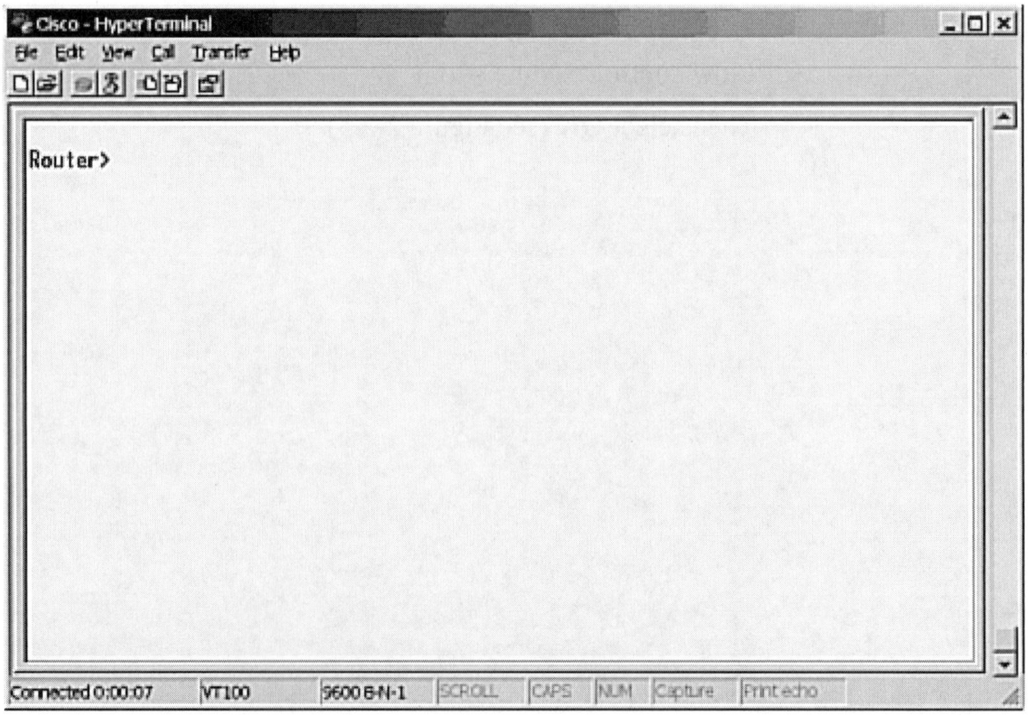

If the router responds, then the connection has been successfully completed.

Step 6. Close the session.

To end the console session from a HyperTerminal session, select **File>Exit**.

When the HyperTerminal disconnect warning popup appears, select **Yes** (see Figure 2-2.6).

Figure 2-2.6 HyperTerminal Session Close

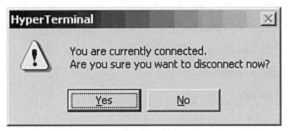

The computer will then ask if the session is to be saved. Select **Yes** (see Figure 2-2.7).

Figure 2-2.7 Saving a HyperTerminal Session

Step 7. Reopen the HyperTerminal connection, as shown previously in Step 2.

    A.   At the Connection Description popup, select **Cancel**.

    B.   To open the saved console session from HyperTerminal, select **File>Open**.

           The saved session will appear. By double-clicking on the name, the connection opens without reconfiguring it each time.

Step 8. Configure host name and passwords on the GAD .

Enter **enable** at the user mode prompt.

```
Router>enable
Router#configure terminal
Router(config)#hostname GAD
GAD(config)#enable secret class
GAD(config)#line console 0
GAD(config-line)#password cisco
GAD(config-line)#login
```

```
GAD(config-line)#line vty 0 4
GAD(config-line)#password cisco
GAD(config-line)#login
GAD(config-line)#exit
GAD(config)#
```

Step 9. From the global configuration mode, configure interface Serial 0 (refer to Appendix C) on router GAD.

```
GAD(config)#interface serial 0
GAD(config-if)#ip address 172.17.0.1 255.255.0.0
GAD(config-if)#clock rate 64000
GAD(config-if)#no shutdown
GAD(config-if)#exit
```

Step 10. Configure the Fast Ethernet 0 interface on router GAD.

```
GAD(config)#interface fastethernet 0
GAD(config-if)#ip address 172.16.0.1 255.255.0.0
GAD(config-if)#no shutdown
GAD(config-if)#exit
```

Step 11. Configure the IP host statements on router GAD.

```
GAD(config)#ip host BMH 172.18.0.1 172.17.0.2
```

Step 12. Configure RIP routing on router GAD.

```
GAD(config)#router rip
GAD(config-router)#network 172.16.0.0
GAD(config-router)#network 172.17.0.0
GAD(config-router)#exit
GAD(config)#exit
```

Step 13. Save the GAD router configuration.

```
GAD#copy running-config startup-config
Destination filename [startup-config]?[Enter]
```

Step 14. Configure host name and passwords on the BHM router.

Enter **enable** at the user mode prompt.

```
Router>enable
Router#configure terminal
Router(config)#hostname BHM
BHM(config)#enable secret class
```

```
BHM(config)#line console 0
BHM(config-line)#password cisco
BHM(config-line)#login
BHM(config-line)#line vty 0 4
BHM(config-line)#password cisco
BHM(config-line)#login
BHM(config-line)#exit
BHM(config)#
```

Step 15. From the global configuration mode, configure interface Serial 0 (refer to Appendix C) on router BHM.

```
BHM(config)#interface serial 0
BHM(config-if)#ip address 172.17.0.2 255.255.0.0
BHM(config-if)#no shutdown
BHM(config-if)#exit
```

Step 16. Configure the Fast Ethernet 0 Interface on router BHM.

```
BHM(config)#interface fastethernet 0
BHM(config-if)#ip address 172.18.0.1 255.255.0.0
BHM(config-if)#no shutdown
BHM(config-if)#exit
```

Step 17. Configure the IP host statements on router BHM.

```
BHM(config)#ip host GAD 172.16.0.1 172.17.0.1
```

Step 18. Configure RIP routing on router BHM.

```
BHM(config)#router rip
BHM(config-router)#network 172.18.0.0
BHM(config-router)#network 172.17.0.0
BHM(config-router)#exit
BHM(config)#exit
```

Step 19. Save the BHM router configuration.

```
BHM# copy running-config startup-config
Destination filename [startup-config]?[Enter]
```

Step 20. Configure the hosts with the proper IP address, subnet mask, and default gateway.

A.   Host connected to router GAD

```
IP address: 172.16.0.2
Subnet mask: 255.255.0.0
Default gateway: 172.16.0.1
```

B.   Host connected to router BHM

```
IP address: 172.18.0.2

Subnet mask: 255.255.0.0

Default gateway: 172.18.0.1
```

Step 21. Verify that the internetwork is functioning by **ping**ing the Fast Ethernet interface of the other router

A.   From the host that is attached to GAD, **ping** the BHM router Fast Ethernet interface. Was the **ping** successful? _____

B.   From the host that is attached to BHM, **ping** the GAD router Fast Ethernet interface. Was the **ping** successful? _____

C.   If the answer is no for either question, troubleshoot the router configurations to find the error. Then do the **ping**s again until the answer to both questions is yes. Finally, **ping** all interfaces in the network.

Step 22. Show the routing tables for each router.

A.   From the enable (privileged EXEC) mode:

Examine the routing table entries by using the **show ip route** command on each router.

B.   What are the entries in the GAD routing table?

_____

C.   What are the entries in the BHM routing table?

_____

Upon completion of the previous steps, log off (by typing **exit**) and turn the router off. Then remove and store the cables and adapter.

Step 1. Configure the routers.

On the routers, configure the host names, console, virtual terminal, and enable passwords. Next, configure the Serial (IP address and clock rate) and Fast Ethernet (IP address) interfaces. Finally, configure IP host names. If you have problems performing the basic configuration, refer to Lab 2-2, "Review of Basic Router Configuration with RIP (TI 1.2.3)." You can also configure optional interface descriptions and message of the day banners. Be sure to save the configurations you just created.

Step 2. Configure the routing protocol on the GAD router.

Go to the proper command mode and configure RIP routing on the GAD router according to Table 2-5.1.

Step 3. Save the GAD router configuration.

Anytime that changes are correctly made to the running configuration, you should save them to the startup configuration. Otherwise, if you reload or power cycle the router, you will lose the changes that are not in the startup configuration.

Step 4. Configure the routing protocol on the BHM router.

Go to the proper command mode and configure RIP routing on the BHM router according to Table 2-5.1.

Step 5. Save the BHM router configuration.

Step 6. Configure the hosts with the proper IP address, subnet mask, and default gateway.

Step 7. Verify that the internetwork is functioning by **ping**ing the Fast Ethernet interface of the other router.

A.   From the host that is attached to GAD, **ping** the other host that is attached to the BHM router. Was the **ping** successful? _____

B.   From the host that is attached to BHM, **ping** the other host that is attached to the GAD router. Was the **ping** successful? _____

C.   If the answer is no for either question, troubleshoot the router configurations to find the error. Then do the **ping**s again until the answer to both questions is yes.

Step 8. Show the **debug ip** command options.

A.   At the privileged EXEC mode prompt, type **debug ip ?**.

B.   Which routing protocols have debug commands?

_____

_____

Step 9. Show the **debug ip rip** options.

A.   At the privileged EXEC mode prompt, type **debug ip rip ?**.

B.   How many options are available for **debug ip rip ?**? _____

Step 10. Show the RIP routing updates.

    A.   From the enable (privileged EXEC) mode, examine the routing table entries by using the **debug ip rip** command on each router.

    B.   What three operations that take place are listed in the RIP debug statements?

    _____   _____   _____

    C.   Turn off debugging by typing either **no debug ip rip** or **undebug all**.

Step 11. Enable RIP version 2 routing on the GAD router only.

Enable version 2 of the RIP routing protocol on the GAD router only.

Step 12. Start the debug function again on the GAD router.

    A.   Does a problem occur now that RIP version 2 is configured on the GAD router? _____

    B.   What is the problem?

    _____

Step 13. Clear the routing table.

    A.   Instead of waiting for the routes to time out, type **clear ip route ***. Then type **show ip route**.

    B.   What has happened to the routing table?

    _____

    C.   Will the routing table be updated to include RIP routes if the debug output says the update is ignored? _____

Step 14. Start the debug RIP function.

    A.   Start the debug RIP function on the BHM router again by typing **debug ip rip**.

    B.   Does a problem occur now that the GAD router is configured with RIP Version 2?_____

    C.   What is the problem?

    _____

Step 15. Clear the routing table.

    A.   Instead of waiting for the routes to time out, type **clear ip route ***. Then type **show ip route**.

    B.   What has happened to the routing table?

    _____

C.   Will the routing table be updated to include RIP routes if the update is from RIP version 2? _____

D.   Turn off debugging by typing either **no debug ip rip** or **undebug all**.

Step 16. Enable RIP version 2 routing on the BHM router.

Enable RIP version 2 on the BHM router.

Step 17. Use the debug function to see packet traffic on a router.

A.   Use the debug function to see packet traffic on the BHM router by typing **debug ip packet** at the privileged EXEC mode.

B.   When an RIP update is sent, how many source addresses are used?

_____

C.   Why are multiple source addresses used?

_____

D.   What is the source address that is used?

_____

E.   Why is this address used?

_____

Step 18. Start the **debug rip database** function again on the BHM router.

A.   Start the RIP database debugging by typing **debug ip rip database**. Then clear the routing table by typing **clear ip route ***.

B.   Are the old routes in the table deleted?

_____

C.   Are new routes added back into the table?

_____

D.   What does the last entry in the debug output say?

_____

E.   Turn off debugging by typing either **no debug ip rip** or **undebug all**

Step 19. Use the **debug events** function to see routing updates.

A.   Use the debug function to see routing updates by typing **debug ip rip events** in privileged EXEC mode on the BHM router.

B.   What interfaces are the routing updates sent on?

_____

C.   How many routes are in the routing updates that are being sent?

_____

D.   Upon completion of the previous steps, log off (by typing **exit**) and turn the router off. Then remove and store the cables and adapter.

CCNA 3

Chapter 3: Single-Area OSPF

The following table maps the numbering scheme that is used in this chapter's labs to the Target Indicators (TIs) that are used in the online curriculum.

Lab Companion Numbering	Online Curriculum TI
Lab 3-1	2.3.1
Lab 3-2	2.3.2
Lab 3-3	2.3.3
Lab 3-4	2.3.4
Lab 3-5	2.3.5
Lab 3-6	2.3.6

Lab 3-1 Configuring the OSPF Routing Process (TI 2.3.1)

Figure 3-1.1 Topology for Lab 3-1

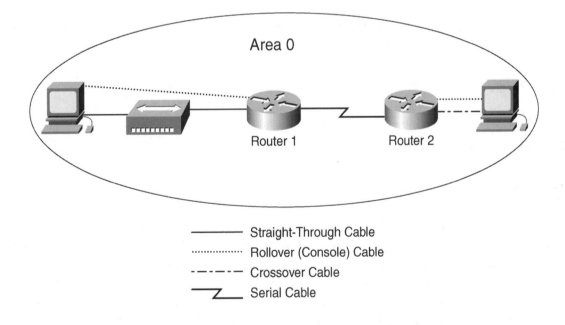

Table 3-1.1   Lab Equipment Configuration

Router Designation	Router Name	Routing Protocol	Network Statements
Router 1	BERLIN	OSPF	192.168.1.128 192.168.15.0
Router 2	ROME	OSPF	192.168.15.0 192.168.0.0

The enable secret password for both routers is **class**.

The enable, VTY, and console password for both routers is **cisco**.

Table 3-1.2   Lab Equipment Interface/IP Address Configurations

Router Designation	Fast Ethernet 0 Address/Subnet Mask	Interface Type Serial 0	Serial 0 Address/Subnet Mask	IP Host Table Entry
Router 1	192.168.1.129/26	DCE	192.168.15.1/30	ROME
Router 2	192.168.0.1/24	DTE	192.168.15.2/30	BERLIN

The interface type and address/subnet mask for the serial 1 interface on both routers is not applicable for this lab.

The IP Host Table Entry column contents indicate the names of the other routers in the IP host table.

Objectives

- Set up an IP addressing scheme for OSPF area 0.
- Configure and verify OSPF routing.

Background/Preparation

Cable a network that is similar to the one in Figure 3-1.1. You can use any router that meets the interface requirements in Figure 3-1.1 (that is, 800, 1600, 1700, 2500, and 2600 routers or a combination). Refer to the information in Appendix C, "Router Interface Summary Chart," to correctly specify the interface identifiers based on the equipment in your lab. The 1721 series routers produced the configuration output in this lab. Another router might produce slightly different output. You should execute the following steps on each router unless you are specifically instructed otherwise. Start a HyperTerminal session.

Implement the procedure documented in Appendix A, "Erasing and Reloading the Router," before you continue with this lab.

Step 1. Configure the routers.

On the routers, enter the global configuration mode and configure the host name as shown in Table 3-1.1. Then configure the console, virtual terminal, and enable passwords. Next, configure the interfaces according to Table 3-1.2. Finally, configure the IP host names. Do not configure the routing protocol until you are specifically told to. If you have problems configuring the router basics, refer to Lab 2-2, "Review of Basic Router Configuring with RIP (TI 1.2.3)."

Note: The command **ip subnet-zero** may need to be added because of the use of the ZERO subnet with VLSM on the 192.168.1.0/30 and 192.168.1.128/26 networks.

Step 2. Save the configuration information from the privileged EXEC command mode.

```
BERLIN# copy running-config startup-config

Destination filename [startup-config]? [Enter]
```

Why save the running configuration to the startup configuration?

_____

_____

Step 3. Configure the hosts with the proper IP address, subnet mask, and default gateway.

A.   Each workstation should be able to **ping** the attached router. Troubleshoot as necessary. Hint: Remember to assign a specific IP address and default gateway to the workstation. If you are running Windows 98, check using **Start>Run>winipcfg**. If you are running Windows 2000, check using **ipconfig** in a DOS window.

B.   At this point, the workstations will not be able to communicate with each other. The following steps will demonstrate the process that is required to get communication working while using OSPF as the routing protocol.

Step 4. View the router's configuration and interface information.

A.   At the privileged EXEC mode prompt, type the following:

```
BERLIN#show running-config
```

B.   Using the **show ip interface brief** command, check the status of each interface.

C.   What is the state of the interfaces on each router?

BERLIN:

Fast Ethernet 0: _____

Serial 0: _____

Serial 1: _____

ROME:

Fast Ethernet 0: _____

Serial 0: _____

D.   **Ping** from one of the connected serial interfaces to the other.

Was the **ping** successful?

_____

E.   If the **ping** was not successful, troubleshoot the router configuration until the **ping** is successful.

Step 5. Configure OSPF routing on router BERLIN.

A.   Configure an OSPF routing process on router BERLIN. Use OSPF process number 1 and ensure that all networks are in area 0.

```
BERLIN(config)#router ospf 1
BERLIN(config-router)#network 192.168.1.128 0.0.0.63 area 0
BERLIN(config-router)#network 192.168.15.0 0.0.0.3 area 0
BERLIN(config-router)#end
```

B.   Examine the routers that are running configurations files.

C.   Did the IOS version automatically add any lines under router OSPF 1?

_____

D.   If so, what did it add?

_____

E.   If there were no changes to the running configuration, type the following commands:

```
BERLIN(config)#router ospf 1
BERLIN(config-router)#log-adjacency-changes
BERLIN(config-router)#end
```

F.   Show the routing table for the BERLIN router:

```
BERLIN#show ip route
```

G.   Do entries exist in the routing table? _____

H.   Why?

_____

Step 6. Configure OSPF routing on router ROME.

A.   Configure an OSPF routing process on router ROME. Use OSPF process number 1 and ensure that all networks are in area 0.

```
ROME(config)#router ospf 1
ROME(config-router)#network 192.168.1.0 0.0.0.255 area 0
ROME(config-router)#network 192.168.15.0 0.0.0.3 area 0
ROME(config-router)#end
```

B.   Examine the ROME router running configuration files.

C.   Did the IOS version automatically add lines under router OSPF 1?

_____

D.   If so, what did it add?

_____

E.   If there were no changes to the running configuration, type the following commands:

```
ROME(config)#router ospf 1
ROME(config-router)#log-adjacency-changes
ROME(config-router)#end
```

F.   Show the routing table for the ROME router.

```
ROME#show ip route
```

G.   Are there OSPF entries in the routing table now?

_____

H.   What is the metric value of the OSPF route?

_____

I.   What is the VIA address in the OSPF route?

_____

J.   Are routes to all networks shown in the routing table?

_____

K.   What does the O mean in the first column of the routing table?

_____

Step 7. Test network connectivity.

Ping the BERLIN host from the ROME host. Was it successful? _____

If not, troubleshoot as necessary.

After you complete the previous steps, log off (by typing **exit**) and turn the router off. Then remove and store the cables and adapter.

Lab 3-2   Configuring OSPF with Loopback Addresses (TI 2.3.2)

Figure 3-2.1 Topology for Lab 3-2

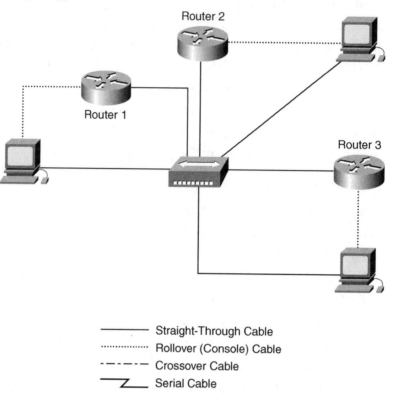

———————	Straight-Through Cable
················	Rollover (Console) Cable
– – – – –	Crossover Cable
——Z——	Serial Cable

Table 3-2.1   Lab Equipment Configuration: Part I

Router Designation	Router Name	Routing Protocol	OSPF Priority	Network Statements
Router 1	London	OSPF	1	192.168.1.0
Router 2	Ottawa	OSPF	1	192.168.1.0
Router 3	Brasilia	OSPF	1	192.168.1.0

The enable secret password for all routers is **class**.

The enable, VTY, and console passwords for each router are **cisco**.

Table 3-2.2   Lab Equipment Configuration: Part II

Router Designation	Fast Ethernet 0 Address/Subnet Mask	Loopback Interface/Subnet Mask	IP Host Table Entry
Router 1	192.168.1.1/24	192.168.31.11/32	Ottawa, Brasilia
Router 2	192.168.1.2/24	192.168.31.22/32	London, Brasilia

Router Designation	Fast Ethernet 0 Address/Subnet Mask	Loopback Interface/Subnet Mask	IP Host Table Entry
Router 3	192.168.1.3/24	192.168.31.33/32	London, Ottawa

The IP Host Table Entry column contents indicate the names of the other routers in the IP host table.

Objectives

- Configure routers with a Class C IP addressing scheme.

- Observe the election process for designated routers (DR) and backup designated routers (BDR) on the multiaccess network.

- Configure loopback addresses for OSPF stability.

- Assign each OSPF interface a priority to force the election of a specific router as DR.

Background/Preparation

Cable a network that is similar to the one in Figure 3-2.1. You can use any router that meets the interface requirements in Figure 3-2.1 (that is, 800, 1600, 1700, 2500, and 2600 routers or a combination). Refer to the information in Appendix C to correctly specify the interface identifiers based on the equipment in your lab. The 1721 series routers produced the configuration output in this lab. Another router might produce slightly different output. You should execute the following steps on each router unless you are specifically instructed otherwise. Start a HyperTerminal session.

Implement the procedure documented in Appendix A on all routers before continuing with this lab.

Step 1. Configure the routers.

On the routers, enter the global configuration mode and configure the host name as shown in Table 3-2.1. Then configure the console, virtual terminal, and enable passwords. Next, configure the interfaces and the IP host names according to the Lab Equipment Configuration tables. If you have problems configuring the router basics, refer to Lab 2-2, "Review of Basic Router Configuring with RIP (TI 1.2.3)." Do not configure loopback interfaces and routing protocols yet.

Step 2. Save the configuration information for all the routers.

Why should you save the running configuration to the startup configuration?

Step 3. Configure the hosts with the proper IP address, subnet mask, and default gateway.

Each workstation should be able to **ping** all the attached routers. That is because they are all part of the same subnetwork. Troubleshoot as necessary. Hint: Remember to assign a specific IP address and default gateway to the workstation. If you are running Windows 98, check using **Start>Run>winipcfg**. If you are running Windows 2000, check using **ipconfig** in a DOS window.

Step 4. View the router's configuration and interface information.

A. At the privileged EXEC mode prompt, type **show running-config**.

B. Using the **show ip interface brief** command, check the status of each interface.

C. What is the state of the interfaces on each router?

D. London:

Fast Ethernet 0: _____

Serial 0: _____

Serial 1: _____

E. Ottawa:

Fast Ethernet 0: _____

Serial 0: _____

Serial 1: _____

F. Brasilia:

Fast Ethernet 0: _____

Serial 0: _____

Serial 1: _____

Step 5. Verify connectivity of the routers.

A. **Ping** all the connected Fast Ethernet interfaces from each other.

B. Were the **ping**s successful?

_____

C. If the **ping**s were not successful, troubleshoot the router configuration until the **ping** is successful.

Step 6. Configure OSPF routing on router London.

    A.   Configure an OSPF routing process on router London. Use OSPF process number 1 and ensure that all networks are in area 0.

```
London(config)#router ospf 1
London(config-router)#network 192.168.1.0 0.0.0.255 area 0
London(config-router)#end
```

    B.   Examine the London router running configuration file.

    C.   Did the IOS version automatically add lines under router OSPF 1?

        _____

    D.   If there were no changes to the running configuration, type the following commands:

```
London(config)#router ospf 1
London(config-router)#log-adjacency-changes
London(config-router)#end
```

    E.   Show the routing table for router:

```
London#show ip route
```

    F.   Are entries in the routing table? _____

    G.   Why?

    _____

Step 7. Configure OSPF routing on router Ottawa,

    A.   Configure an OSPF routing process on router Ottawa. Use OSPF process number 1 and ensure that all networks are in area 0.

```
Ottawa(config)#router ospf 1
Ottawa(config-router)#network 192.168.1.0 0.0.0.255 area 0
Ottawa(config-router)#end
```

    B.   Examine the Ottawa router running configuration files.

    C.   Did the IOS version automatically add lines under router OSPF 1?

        _____

    D.   If no changes were made to the running configuration, type the following commands:

```
Ottawa(config)#router ospf 1
Ottawa(config-router)#log-adjacency-changes
Ottawa(config-router)#end
```

Step 8. Configure OSPF routing on router Brasilia.

    A.   Configure an OSPF routing process on router Brasilia. Use OSPF process number 1 and ensure that all networks are in area 0.

```
Brasilia(config)#router ospf 1

Brasilia(config-router)#network 192.168.1.0 0.0.0.255 area 0

Brasilia(config-router)#end
```

    B.   Examine the Brasilia router running configuration files.

           Did the IOS version automatically add lines under router OSPF 1?

           _____

    C.   What did it add?

           _____

    D.   If there were no changes to the running configuration, type the following commands:

```
Brasilia(config)#router ospf 1

Brasilia(config-router)#log-adjacency-changes

Brasilia(config-router)#end
```

Step 9. Test network connectivity.

Ping the Brasilia router from the London router. Was it successful? _____

If not, troubleshoot as necessary.

Step 10. Show OSPF adjacencies.

    A.   Type the command **show ip ospf neighbor** on all routers to verify that the OSPF routing has formed adjacencies.

    B.   Is there a designated router identified?

           _____

    C.   Is there a backup designated router?

           _____

    D.   Type the command **show ip ospf neighbor detail** for more information.

    E.   What is the neighbor priority of 192.168.1.1 from router Brasilia?

           _____

    F.   What interface is identified as being part of area 0?

           _____

Step 11. Configure the loopback interfaces.

Configure the loopback interface on each router to allow for an interface that will not go down due to network change or failure. You can accomplish this by typing **interface loopback #** at the global configuration mode prompt, where the # represents the number of the loopback interface from 0 to 2,147,483,647.

```
London(config)#interface loopback 0
London(config-if)#ip address 192.168.31.11 255.255.255.255
London(config-router)#end


Ottawa(config)#interface loopback 0
Ottawa(config-if)#ip address 192.168.31.22 255.255.255.255
Ottawa(config-router)#end


Brasilia(config)#interface loopback 0
Brasilia(config-if)#ip address 192.168.31.33 255.255.255.255
Brasilia(config-router)#end
```

Step 12. Save the configuration information for all the routers.

After you save the configurations on all the routers, power them down and back up again.

Step 13. Show OSPF adjacencies.

A.   Type the command **show ip ospf neighbor** on all routers to verify that the OSPF routing has formed adjacencies.

B.   Is a designated router identified?

     _____

C.   What are the Router ID and link address of the DR?

     _____

D.   Is there a backup designated router?

     _____

E.   What are the Router ID and link address of the BDR? _____

     _____

F.   What is the third router referred to as?

     _____

G.   What is that router's ID and link address?

     _____

H.   Type the command **show ip ospf neighbor detail** for more information.

I.   What is the neighbor priority of 192.168.1.1 from router Brasilia?

_____

J.   Which interface is identified as being part of area 0?

_____

Step 14. Verify OSPF interface configuration.

A.   Type **show ip ospf interface fastethernet 0** on the London router.

B.   What is the OSPF state of the interface?

_____

C.   What is the default priority of the interface?_____

D.   What is the network type of the interface?

_____

Step 15. Configure London to always be the DR.

A.   To ensure that the London router always becomes the DR for this multiaccess segment, you must set the OSPF priority. London is the most powerful router in the network, so it is best suited to become the DR. Giving London's loopback a higher IP address is not advised because the numbering system has advantages for troubleshooting. Also, London is not to act as the DR for all segments to which it might belong.

B.   Set the priority of the interface to 50 on the London router only.

```
London(config)# interface fastethernet 0/0
London(config-if)# ip ospf priority  50
London(config-router)# end
```

C.   Display the priority for Interface fastethernet 0/0.

```
London# show ip ospf interface fastethernet 0/0
```

Step 16. Watch the election process.

A.   To watch the OSPF election process, restart all the routers using the reload command. Be sure to save the running config before restarting the routers. Another option is to use the **shutdown** command to disable the FastEthernet interfaces on all routers and then use the **no shutdown** command to re-enable them. As soon as the router prompt is available, type the following:

```
Ottawa>enable
Ottawa#debug ip ospf events
```

B.   Which router was elected DR?

_____

C.   Which router was elected BDR?

_____

D.   Why?

_____

E.   To turn off all debugging, type **undebug all**.

Step 17. Show OSPF adjacencies.

A.   Type the command **show ip ospf neighbor** on the Ottawa router to verify
        that the OSPF routing has formed adjacencies.

B.   What is the priority of the DR?

_____

After you complete the previous steps, log off (by typing **exit**) and turn the router off.
Then remove and store the cables and adapter.

Lab 3-3   Modifying OSPF Cost Metric (TI 2.3.3)

Figure 3-3.1 Topology for Lab 3-3

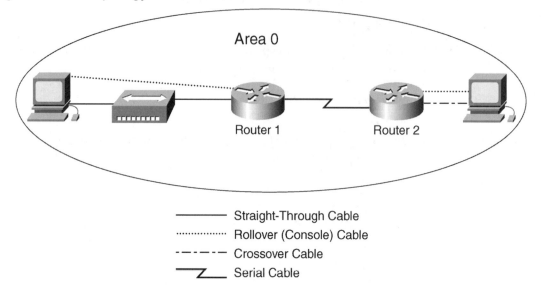

Table 3-3.1   Lab Equipment Configuration: Part I

Router Designation	Router Name	Routing Protocol	Network Statements
Router 1	Cairo	OSPF	192.168.1.0
Router 2	Moscow	OSPF	192.168.1.0 192.168.0.0

The enable secret password for both routers is **class**.

The enable, VTY, and console passwords for both routers are **cisco**.

Table 3-3.2   Lab Equipment Configuration: Part II

Router Designation	Fast Ethernet 0 Address/Subnet Mask	Interface Type Serial 0	Serial 0 Address/Subnet Mask	IP Host Table Entry
Router 1	192.168.1.129/26	DCE	192.168.1.1/30	Moscow
Router 2	192.168.0.1/24	DTE	192.168.1.2/30	Cairo

The interface type and address/subnet mask for the serial 1 interface on both routers are not applicable for this lab.

The IP Host Table Entry column contents indicate the names of the other routers in the IP host table.

Objectives

- Set up an IP addressing scheme for the OSPF area.

- Configure and verify OSPF routing.

- Modify the OSPF cost metric on an interface.

Background/Preparation

Cable a network that is similar to the one in Figure 3-3.1. You can use any router that meets the interface requirements in Figure 3-3.1 (that is, 800, 1600, 1700, 2500, and 2600 routers or a combination). Refer to the information in Appendix C to correctly specify the interface identifiers based on the equipment in your lab. The 1721 series routers produced the configuration output in this lab. Another router might produce slightly different output. You should execute the following steps on each router unless you are specifically instructed otherwise.

Start a HyperTerminal session.

Implement the procedure documented in Appendix A on all routers before you continue with this lab.

Step 1. Configure the routers.

On the routers, enter the global configuration mode and configure the host name, console, virtual terminal, and enable passwords. Next, configure the interfaces and IP host names according to the Lab Equipment Configuration tables. Do not configure the routing protocol until you are specifically told to. If you have problems configuring the router basics, refer to Lab 2-2, "Review of Basic Router Configuring with RIP (TI 1.2.3)."

Note: The command **ip subnet-zero** may need to be added because of the use of the ZERO subnet with VLSM on the 192.168.1.0/30 and 192.168.1.128/26 networks.

Step 2. Save the configuration information from the privileged EXEC command mode.

```
Cairo# copy running-config startup-config

Destination filename [startup-config]?[Enter]

Moscow# copy running-config startup-config

Destination filename [startup-config]?[Enter]
```

Why should you save the running configuration to the startup configuration?

_____

Step 3. Configure the hosts with the proper IP address, subnet mask, and default gateway.

A.   Each workstation should be able to **ping** the attached router. Troubleshoot as necessary. Hint: Remember to assign a specific IP address and default gateway to the workstation. If you are running Windows 98, check using **Start**>**Run**>**winipcfg**. If you are running Windows 2000, check using **ipconfig** in a DOS window.

      B.   At this point, the workstations will not be able to communicate with each other. The following steps demonstrate the process that is required to get communication working while using OSPF as the routing protocol.

Step 4. View the router's configuration and interface information.

      A.   At the privileged EXEC mode prompt, type the following:

```
Cairo#show running-config
```

      B.   Using the **show ip interface brief** command, check the status of each interface.

      C.   What is the state of the interfaces on each router?

      D.   Cairo:

           Fast Ethernet 0: _____

           Serial 0: _____

      E.   Moscow:

           Fast Ethernet 0: _____

           Serial 0: _____

      F.   **Ping** from one of the connected router serial interfaces to the other.

      G.   Was the **ping** successful? _____

      H.   If the **ping** was not successful, troubleshoot the router configuration until the **ping** is successful.

Step 5. Configure OSPF routing on router Cairo.

      A.   Configure OSPF routing on each router. Use OSPF process number 1 and ensure that all networks are in area 0.

```
Cairo(config)#router ospf 1
Cairo(config-router)#network 192.168.1.128 0.0.0.63 area 0
Cairo(config-router)#network 192.168.1.0 0.0.0.3 area 0
Cairo(config-router)#end
```

      B.   Examine the running configuration file.

      C.   Did the IOS version automatically add lines under router OSPF 1?

           _____

      D.   What did it add?

           _____

           If there were no changes to the running configuration, type the following commands:

```
Cairo(config)#router ospf 1
Cairo(config-router)#log-adjacency-changes
Cairo(config-router)#end
```

E.   Show the routing table for the Cairo router.

Cairo#**show ip route**

F.   Do entries exist in the routing table? _____

G.   Why?

_____

Step 6. Configure OSPF routing on router Moscow.

A.   Configure OSPF routing on each router. Use OSPF process number 1 and ensure that all networks are in area 0.

Moscow(config)#**router ospf 1**

Moscow(config-router)#**network 192.168.0.0 0.0.0.255 area 0**

Moscow(config-router)#**network 192.168.1.0 0.0.0.3 area 0**

Moscow(config-router)#**end**

B.   Examine the running configuration file.

C.   Did the IOS version automatically add lines under router OSPF 1?

_____

D.   If there were no changes to the running configuration, type the following commands:

Moscow(config)#**router ospf 1**

Moscow(config-router)#**log-adjacency-changes**

Moscow(config-router)#**end**

Step 7. Show the routing table entries.

A.   Show the routing table entries for the Cairo router.

Cairo#**show ip route**

B.   Does the routing table have OSPF entries now?

_____

C.   What is the metric value of the OSPF route?

_____

D.   What is the VIA address in the OSPF route?

_____

E.   Are routes to all networks shown in the routing table?

_____

F.   What does the O mean in the first column of the routing table?

_____

Step 8. Test network connectivity.

Ping the Cairo host from the Moscow host. Was it successful? _____

If not, troubleshoot as necessary.

Step 9. Look at the OSPF cost on the Cairo router interfaces.

  A. Show the properties of the Cairo router serial and Fast Ethernet interfaces by using the **show interfaces** command.

  B. What is the default bandwidth of the interfaces?

  C. Serial interface _____

  D. Fast Ethernet interface _____

  E. Calculate the OSPF cost.

  F. Serial interface _____

  G. Fast Ethernet interface_____

Link Bandwidth	Default OSPF Cost
56 Kbps	1785
T1	64
10-Mbps Ethernet	10
16-Mbps Token Ring	6
FDDI/Fast Ethernet	1

Step 10. Record the OSPF cost of the serial and Fast Ethernet interfaces.

  A. Using the **show ip ospf interface** command, record the OSPF cost of the serial and Fast Ethernet interfaces.

  B. OSPF cost of serial interface: _____

  C. OSPF cost of Ethernet interface:_____

  D. Do these agree with the calculations? _____

  E. The clock rate set for the interface should have been 64,000. This is what has been used as a default to this point and specified Lab 2-2, "Review of Basic Router Configuring with RIP (TI 1.2.3)." Therefore, to calculate the cost of this bandwidth, we need to divide 10^8 by 64,000.

Step 11. Manually set the cost on the serial interface.

On the serial interface of the Cairo router, set the OSPF cost to 1562 by typing **ip ospf cost 1562** at the serial interface configuration mode prompt.

Step 12. Verify cost.

Note that it is essential that all connected links agree about the cost for consistent calculation of the SPF in an area.

  A. Verify that the interface OSPF cost was successfully modified.

  B. Reverse the effect of this command by entering the command **no ip ospf cost** in interface configuration mode.

  C. Verify that the default cost for the interface has returned.

D.   Enter the command **bandwidth 2000** at the serial 0 interface configuration mode prompt.

E.   Record the new OSPF cost of the serial interface.

_____

F.   Can the OSPF cost of an Ethernet interface be modified in this way?

_____

G.   You can set the speed on an Ethernet interface. Will this affect the OSPF cost of that interface?

_____

H.   Verify or explain the previous answer.

_____

_____

_____

_____

_____

_____

I.   Reset the bandwidth on the serial interface by using **no bandwidth 2000** at the serial 0 interface configuration mode prompt.

After you complete the previous steps, log off (by typing **exit**) and turn the router off. Then remove and store the cables and adapter.

Lab 3-4   Configuring OSPF Authentication (TI 2.3.4)

Figure 3-4.1 Topology for Lab 3-4

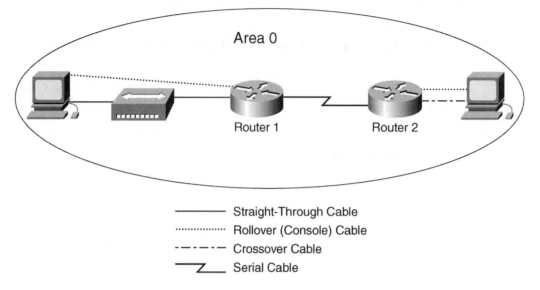

Table 3-4.1   Lab Equipment Configuration: Part I

Router Designation	Router Name	Routing Protocol	Network Statements
Router 1	Dublin	OSPF	192.168.1.0
Router 2	Washington	OSPF	192.168.1.0 192.168.0.0

The enable secret password for both routers is **class**.

The enable, VTY, and console password for both routers is **cisco**.

Table 3-4.2 Lab Equipment Configuration: Part II

Router Designation	Fast Ethernet 0 Address/ Subnet Mask	Inter-face Type Serial 0	Serial 0 Address/ Subnet Mask	Loopback 0 Address/ Subnet Mask	IP Host Table Entry
Router 1	192.168.1.129/26	DCE	192.168.1.1/30	192.168.31.11/32	Washington
Router 2	192.168.0.1/24	DTE	192.168.1.2/30	192.168.31.22/32	Dublin

The interface type and address/subnet mask for the serial 1 interface on both routers is not applicable for this lab.

The IP Host Table Entry column contents indicate the names of the other routers in the IP host table.

Objectives

- Set up an IP addressing scheme for the OSPF area.

- Configure and verify OSPF routing.

- Introduce OSPF authentication into the area.

Background/Preparation

Cable a network that is similar to the one in Figure 3-4.1. You can use any router that meets the interface requirements in Figure 3-4.1 (that is, 800, 1600, 1700, 2500, and 2600 routers or a combination). Refer to the information in Appendix C to correctly specify the interface identifiers based on the equipment in your lab. The 1721 series routers produced the configuration output in this lab. Another router might produce slightly different output. You should execute the following steps on each router unless you are specifically instructed otherwise.

Start a HyperTerminal session.

Implement the procedure documented in Appendix A on all routers before you continue with this lab.

Step 1. Configure the routers.

On the routers, enter the global configuration mode and configure the host name, console, virtual terminal, and enable passwords. Next, configure the interfaces and IP host names according to the Lab Equipment Configuration tables. Do not configure the routing protocol until you are specifically told to. If you have problems configuring the router basics, refer to Lab 2-2, "Review of Basic Router Configuring with RIP (TI 1.2.3)."

Note: The command **ip subnet-zero** may need to be added because of the use of the ZERO subnet with VLSM on the 192.168.1.0/30 and 192.168.1.128/26 networks.

Step 2. Save the configuration information from the privileged EXEC command mode.

```
Dublin# copy running-config startup-config
Destination filename [startup-config]? [Enter]


Washington# copy running-config startup-config
Destination filename [startup-config]? [Enter]
```

Why should you save the running configuration to the startup configuration?

_____

Step 3. Configure the hosts with the proper IP address, subnet mask, and default gateway.

    A.   Each workstation should be able to **ping** the attached router. Troubleshoot as necessary. Hint: Remember to assign a specific IP address and default gateway to the workstation. If you are running Windows 98, check using **Start>Run>winipcfg**. If you are running Windows 2000, check using **ipconfig** in a DOS window.

B.   At this point, the workstations will not be able to communicate with each other. The following steps demonstrate the process required to get communication working by using OSPF as the routing protocol.

Step 4. Verify connectivity.

A.   **Ping** from one of the connected router serial interfaces to the other.

B.   Was the **ping** successful?

_____

C.   If the **ping** was not successful, troubleshoot the router's configurations until the **ping** is successful.

Step 5. Configure OSPF routing on both routers.

A.   Configure OSPF routing on each router. Use OSPF process number 1 and ensure that all networks are in area 0. Refer to Lab 3-2, "Configuring OSPF with Loopback Addresses (TI 2.3.2)," for a review on configuring OSPF routing.

B.   Examine the Dublin router running the configuration file. Did the IOS version automatically add lines under router OSPF 1? _____

C.   Show the routing table for the Dublin router.

```
Dublin#show ip route
```

D.   Do entries exist in the routing table?

E.   Why?

_____

Step 6. Test network connectivity.

Ping the Dublin host from the Washington host. Was it successful? _____

If not, troubleshoot as necessary.

Step 7. Set up OSPF authentication.

OSPF authentication is being established on the routers in the network. First, introduce authentication only on the Dublin router.

A.   In interface configuration mode on serial 0, enter the command **ip ospf message-digest-key 1 md5 7 asecret.**

```
Dublin(config)#interface Serial 0

Dublin(config-if)#ip ospf message-digest-key 1 md5 ?

<0-7> Encryption type (0 for not yet encrypted, 7 for
  proprietary)

Dublin(config-if)#ip ospf message-digest-key 1 md5 7 ?
```

```
       LINE The OSPF password (key)
       Dublin(config-if)#ip ospf message-digest-key 1 md5 7
          asecret
```

B.   What is the OSPF password being used for md5 authentication?

_____

C.   What encryption type is being used?

_____

Step 8. Enable OSPF authentication in this area, area 0.

```
       Dublin(config-if)#router ospf 1
       Dublin(config-router)#area 0 authentication message-digest
```

A.   Wait for a few seconds. Does the router generate output? _____

B.   Enter the command **show ip ospf neighbor**.

C.   Are there OSPF neighbors?

_____.

D.   Examine the routing table by entering **show ip route**.

E.   Are there OSPF routes in the Dublin router routing table?

F.   Can the Dublin host **ping** the Washington host? _____

G.   Enter configuration commands, one per line. End with **Ctl+Z**.

```
       Washington#configure terminal
       Washington(config)#interface serial 0
       Washington(config-if)#ip ospf message-digest-key 1 md5 7
          asecret
       Washington(config-if)#router ospf 1
       Washington(config-router)#area 0 authentication message-
          digest
```

H.   Verify that there is an OSPF neighbor by entering the **show ip ospf neighbor** command.

I.   Show the routing table by typing **show ip route**.

J.   **Ping** the Washington host from Dublin. If it is not successful, troubleshoot as necessary.

After you complete the previous steps, log off (by typing **exit**) and turn the router off. Then remove and store the cables and adapter.

Lab 3-5   Configuring OSPF Timers (TI 2.3.5)

Figure 3-5.1 Topology for Lab 3-5

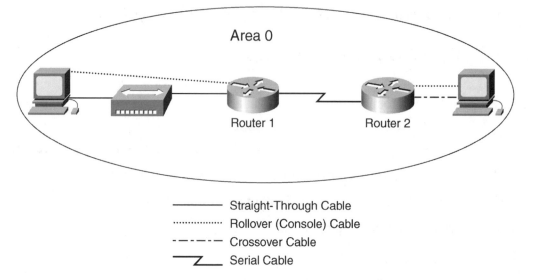

Table 3-5.1   Lab Equipment Configuration: Part I

Router Designation	Router Name	Routing Protocol	Network Statements
Router 1	Sydney	OSPF	192.168.1.0
Router 2	Rome	OSPF	192.168.1.0 192.168.0.0

The enable secret password for both routers is **class**.

The enable, VTY, and console password for both routers is **cisco**.

Table 3-5.2   Lab Equipment Configuration: Part II

Router Designation	Fast Ethernet 0 Address/ Subnet Mask	Inter-face Type Serial 0	Serial 0 Address/ Subnet Mask	Loopback 0 Address/ Subnet Mask	IP Host Table Entry
Router 1	192.168.1.129/26	DCE	192.168.1.1/30	192.168.31.11/32	Rome
Router 2	192.168.0.1/24	DTE	192.168.1.2/30	192.168.31.22/32	Sydney

The interface type and address/subnet mask for the serial 1 interface on both routers is not applicable for this lab.

The IP Host Table Entry column contents indicate the names of the other routers in the IP host table.

Objectives

- Set up an IP addressing scheme for the OSPF area.

- Configure and verify OSPF routing.

- Modify OSPF interface timers to adjust efficiency of the network.

Background/Preparation

Cable a network that is similar to the one in Figure 3-5.1. You can use any router that meets the interface requirements in Figure 3-5.1 (that is, 800, 1600, 1700, 2500, and 2600 routers or a combination). Refer to the information in Appendix C to correctly specify the interface identifiers based on the equipment in your lab. The 1721 series routers produced the configuration output in this lab. Another router might produce slightly different output. You should execute the following steps on each router unless you are specifically instructed otherwise. Start a HyperTerminal session.

Implement the procedure documented in Appendix A on all routers before you continue with this lab.

Step 1. Configure the routers.

On the routers, enter the global configuration mode and configure the host name, console, virtual terminal, and enable passwords. Next, configure the interfaces and IP host names according to the Lab Equipment Configuration tables. Do not configure the routing protocol until you are specifically told to. If you have problems configuring the router basics, refer to Lab 2-2, "Review of Basic Router Configuring with RIP (TI 1.2.3)."

Note: The command **ip subnet-zero** may need to be added because of the use of the ZERO subnet with VLSM on the 192.168.1.0/30 and 192.168.1.128/26 networks.

Step 2. Save the configuration information from the privileged EXEC command mode.

```
Sydney# copy running-config startup-config

Destination filename [startup-config]? [Enter]


Rome# copy running-config startup-config

Destination filename [startup-config]? [Enter]
```

Why should you save the running configuration to the startup configuration?

_____

Step 3. Configure the hosts with the proper IP address, subnet mask, and default gateway.

   A.   Each workstation should be able to **ping** the attached router. Troubleshoot as necessary. Hint: Remember to assign a specific IP address and default gateway to the workstation. If you are running Windows 98, check using **Start**>**Run**>**winipcfg**. If you are running Windows 2000, check using **ipconfig** in a DOS window.

B.   At this point, the workstations will not be able to communicate with each other. The following steps demonstrate the process that is required to get communication working by using OSPF as the routing protocol.

Step 4. Verify connectivity.

A.   **Ping** from one of the connected serial interfaces to the other.

B.   Was the **ping** successful?

_____

C.   If the **ping** was not successful, troubleshoot the router configurations until the **ping** is successful.

Step 5. Configure OSPF routing on both routers.

A.   Configure OSPF routing on each router. Use OSPF process number 1 and ensure that all networks are in area 0. Refer to Lab 3-2, "Configuring OSPF with Loopback Addresses (TI 2.3.2)," for a review on configuring OSPF routing.

B.   Did the IOS version automatically add lines under router OSPF 1?

_____

C.   Show the routing table for the Sydney router.

```
Sydney#show ip route
```

D.   Do entries exist in the routing table? _____

Step 6. Test network connectivity.

Ping the Sydney host from the Rome host. Was it successful? _____

If not, troubleshoot as necessary.

Step 7. Observe OSPF traffic.

A.   At privileged EXEC mode, type the command **debug ip ospf events** and observe the output.

B.   How frequently are Hello messages sent?

_____

C.   Where are Hello messages coming from?

_____

D.   Turn off debugging by typing **no debug ip ospf events** or **undebug all**.

Step 8. Show interface timer information.

A.   Show the hello and dead interval timers on the Sydney router Ethernet and serial interfaces by entering the command **show ip ospf interface** in privileged EXEC mode.

B. Record the Hello and Dead interval timers for these interfaces:

C. Hello interval:

_____

D. Dead interval:

_____

E. What is the purpose of the dead interval?

_____

Step 9. Modify the Sydney router OSPF timers.

A. Modify the Hello and Dead interval timers to smaller values to try to improve performance. On the Sydney router only, enter the commands **ip ospf hello-interval 5** and **ip ospf dead-interval 20** for interface serial 0.

```
Sydney(config)#interface Serial 0
Sydney(config-if)#ip ospf hello-interval 5
Sydney(config-if)#ip ospf dead-interval 20
```

B. Wait for a minute and then enter the command **show ip ospf neighbor**.

C. Do OSPF neighbors exist? _____

Step 10. Examine the routing table.

A. Examine the Sydney router routing table by entering **show ip route**.

B. Do OSPF routes exist in the table?

_____

C. Can the Sydney host **ping** the Rome host?

_____

Step 11. Look at the OSPF data transmissions.

A. Enter the command **debug ip ospf events** in privileged EXEC mode.

B. Is there an issue that is identified?

_____

C. If there is, what is the issue?

_____

Step 12. Check the Rome router routing table status.

A. On the Rome router, check the routing table by typing **show ip route**.

B. Do OSPF routes exist in the table?

_____

Step 13. Set the Rome router interval timers.

    A.   Match the timer values on the Rome serial link with the Sydney router.

```
Rome(config)#interface serial 0
Rome(config-if)#ip ospf hello-interval 5
Rome(config-if)#ip ospf dead-interval 20
```

    B.   Verify the OSPF neighbor by entering the **show ip ospf neighbor** command.

    C.   Show the routing table by typing **show ip route**.

    D.   Do OSPF routes exist in the table?

            _____

    E.   **Ping** the Rome host from Sydney. If this is not successful, troubleshoot the configurations.

Step 14. Reset the router's interval timers to the default values.

Use the no form of the **ip ospf hello-interval** and **the ip ospf dead-interval** to reset the OSPF timers back to their default values.

Step 15. Verify that the interval timers are returned to the default values.

    A.   Use the **show ip ospf interface** command to verify that the timers are reset to their default values.

    B.   Are the values back to the default?

            _____

    C.   If not, repeat step 13 and verify again.

After you complete the previous steps, log off (by typing **exit**) and turn the router off. Then remove and store the cables and adapter.

Lab 3-6 Propagating Default Routes in an OSPF Domain (TI 2.3.6)

Figure 3-6.1 Topology for Lab 3-6

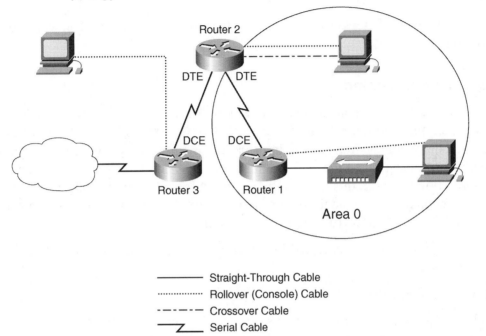

- ———— Straight-Through Cable
- ············· Rollover (Console) Cable
- — — — — Crossover Cable
- ⌐Z— Serial Cable

Table 3-6.1 Lab Equipment Configuration: Part I

Router Designation	Router Name	Routing Protocol	Network Statements	Loopback 0 Address/Subnet Mask
Router 1	Tokyo	OSPF	192.168.1.0	192.168.31.11/32
Router 2	Madrid	OSPF	192.168.1.0 192.168.0.0	192.168.31.22/32

The enable secret password for all routers is **class**.

The enable, VTY, and console passwords for each router are **cisco**.

Table 3-6.2 Lab Equipment Configuration: Part II

Router Designation	Fast Ethernet 0 Address/ Subnet Mask	Interface Type Serial 0	Serial 0 Address/ Subnet Mask	Inter-face Type Serial 1	Serial 1 Address/ Subnet Mask	IP Host Table Entry
Router 1	192.168.1.129/26	DCE	192.168.1.1/30	N/A	N/A	Madrid
Router 2	192.168.0.1/24	DTE	192.168.1.2/30	DTE	200.20.20.2/30	Tokyo

The IP Host Table Entry column contents indicate the names of the other routers in the IP host table.

Objectives

- Set up an IP addressing scheme for the OSPF area.

- Configure and verify OSPF routing.

- Configure the OSPF network so that all hosts in an OSPF area can connect to outside networks.

Background/Preparation

Cable a network that is similar to the one in Figure 3-6.1. You can use any router that meets the interface requirements in Figure 3-6.1 (that is, 800, 1600, 1700, 2500, and 2600 routers or a combination). Refer to the information in Appendix C to correctly specify the interface identifiers based on the equipment in your lab. The 1721 series routers produced the configuration output in this lab. Another router might produce slightly different output. You should execute the following steps on each router unless you are specifically instructed otherwise. Start a HyperTerminal session.

Implement the procedure documented in Appendix A on all routers before you continue with this lab.

Step 1. Configure the ISP router.

Normally, the ISP would configure the ISP router (Router 3). For the purpose of this lab, after you erase the old configuration, configure the ISP router (Router 3) by typing the following:

```
Router>enable
Router#configure terminal
Router(config)#hostname ISP
ISP(config)#line vty 0 4
ISP(config-line)#password cisco
ISP(config-line)#login
ISP(config-line)#interface serial 1
ISP(config-if)#ip address 200.20.20.1 255.255.255.252
ISP(config-if)#clock rate 64000
ISP(config-if)#no shutdown
ISP(config-if)#interface loopback 0
ISP(config-if)#ip address 138.25.6.33 255.255.255.255
ISP(config-if)#exit
ISP(config)#ip route 192.168.1.0 255.255.255.0 200.20.20.2
ISP(config)#ip route 192.168.0.0 255.255.255.0 200.20.20.2
ISP(config)#end
ISP#copy running-config startup-config
Destination filename [startup-config]? [Enter]
Building configuration...
[OK]
ISP#
```

Step 2. Configure the area 0 OSPF routers.

On the routers, enter the global configuration mode and configure the host name, console, virtual terminal, and enable passwords. Next, configure the interfaces and IP host names according to the Lab Equipment Configuration tables. Do not configure the routing protocol until you are specifically told to. If you have problems configuring the router basics, refer to Lab 2-2, "Review of Basic Router Configuring with RIP (TI 1.2.3)."

Step 3. Save the configuration information from the privileged EXEC command mode.

```
Tokyo# copy running-config startup-config

Destination filename [startup-config]? [Enter]


Madrid# copy running-config startup-config

Destination filename [startup-config]? [Enter]
```

Why should you save the running configuration to the startup configuration?

_____

Step 4. Configure the hosts with the proper IP address, subnet mask, and default gateway.

A.   Each workstation should be able to **ping** the attached router. Troubleshoot as necessary. Hint: Remember to assign a specific IP address and default gateway to the workstation. If you are running Windows 98, check using **Start>Run>winipcfg**. If you are running Windows 2000, check using **ipconfig** in a DOS window.

B.   At this point, the workstations will not be able to communicate with each other. The following steps demonstrate the process that is required to get communication working by using OSPF as the routing protocol.

Step 5. Verify connectivity.

A.   **Ping** from the Madrid router to both the Tokyo and ISP routers.

B.   Were the **ping**s successful?

_____

C.   If the **ping** was not successful, troubleshoot the router configurations until the **ping** is successful.

Step 6. Configure OSPF routing on both area 0 routers.

A.   Configure OSPF routing on each router. Use OSPF process number 1 and ensure that all networks are in area 0. Refer to Lab 3-2, "Configuring OSPF with Loopback Addresses (TI 2.3.2)," for a review on configuring OSPF routing.

B.   Did the IOS version automatically add lines under router OSPF 1?

_____

C.   Show the routing table for the Tokyo router.

    Tokyo#**show ip route**

D.   Do entries exist in the routing table? _____

Step 7. Test network connectivity.

Ping the Tokyo host from the Madrid host. Was it successful? _____

If not, troubleshoot as necessary.

Step 8. Observe OSPF traffic.

A.   At privileged EXEC mode, type the command **debug ip ospf events** and observe the output.

B.   Is there OSPF traffic?

       _____

C.   Turn off debugging by typing **no debug ip ospf events** or **undebug all.**

Step 9. Create a default route to the ISP.

On the Madrid router only, type a static default route via the serial 1 interface.

    Madrid(config)#**ip route 0.0.0.0 0.0.0.0 200.20.20.1**

Step 10. Verify the default static route.

A.   Verify the default static route by looking at the Madrid routing table.

B.   Is the default route in the routing table? _____

Step 11. Verify connectivity from the Madrid router.

A.   Verify connectivity from the Madrid router by **ping**ing the ISP serial 1 interface from the Madrid router.

B.   Can the interface be **ping**ed?

       _____

C.   Next, **ping** from a DOS window on the host that is attached to the Madrid router Fast Ethernet interface to the ISP router serial 1 interface.

D.   Can the interface be **ping**ed?

       _____

E.   **Ping** again from the host to the loopback address on the ISP router, which represents the ISP connection to the Internet.

F.   Can the loopback interface be **ping**ed?

       _____

G.   All these **ping**s should be successful. If they are not, troubleshoot the configurations on the host and the Madrid and ISP routers.

Step 12. Verify connectivity from the Tokyo router.

A.   Verify the connection between the ISP and Tokyo by **ping**ing the ISP router serial 1 interface from the Tokyo router.

B.   Can the interface be **ping**ed?

       _____

C.   If yes, why? If not, why not?

       _____

Step 13. Redistribute the static default route.

    A.   Propagate the gateway of last resort to the other routers in the OSPF domain. At the configure router prompt on the Madrid router, type **default-information originate**.

```
Madrid(config-router)#default-information originate
```

    C.   Does a default route now exist on the Tokyo router?

            _____

    D.   What is the address of the gateway of last resort?

            _____

    E.   There is an O*E2 entry in the routing table. What type of route is it?

            _____

    F.   Can the ISP server address at 138.25.6.33 be **ping**ed from both workstations? _____

    G.   If not, troubleshoot both hosts and all three routers.

After you complete the previous steps, log off (by typing **exit**) and turn the router off. Then remove and store the cables and adapter.

CCNA 3

Chapter 4: Enhanced Interior Gateway Routing Protocol (EIGRP)

The following table maps the numbering scheme that is used in this chapter's labs to the Target Indicators (TIs) that are used in the online curriculum.

Lab Companion Numbering	Online Curriculum TI
Lab 4-1	3.2.1
Lab 4-2	3.2.3

Lab 4-1   Configuring EIGRP Routing (TI 3.2.1)

Figure 4-1.1 Topology for Lab 4-1

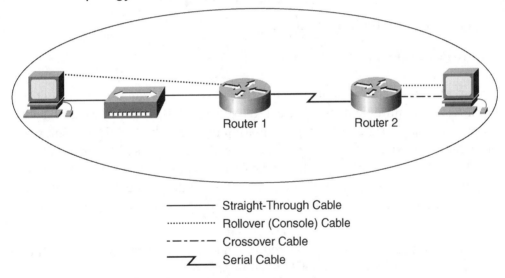

———— Straight-Through Cable
·············· Rollover (Console) Cable
– – – – – Crossover Cable
⌐⌐⌐ Serial Cable

Table 4-1.1   Lab Equipment Configuration: Part I

Router Designation	Router Name	Routing Protocol	Network Statements
Router 1	Paris	EIGRP	192.168.3.0 192.168.2.0
Router 2	Warsaw	EIGRP	192.168.1.0 192.168.2.0

The enable secret password for both routers is **class**.

The enable, VTY, and console password for both routers is **cisco**.

Table 4-1.2   Lab Equipment Configuration: Part II

Router Designation	Fast Ethernet 0 Address/ Subnet Mask	Inter-face Type Serial 0	Serial 0 Address/ Subnet Mask	Loopback 0 Address/ Subnet Mask	IP Host Table Entry
Router 1	192.168.3.1/24	DCE	192.168.2.1/30	192.168.0.2/24	Warsaw
Router 2	192.168.1.1/24	DTE	192.168.2.2/30	No Address	Paris

The interface type and address/subnet mask for the serial 1 interface on both routers is not applicable for this lab.

The IP Host Table Entry column contents indicate the names of the other routers in the IP host table.

Objective

- Set up an IP addressing scheme for the network.

- Configure and verify EIGRP routing.

Background/Preparation

Cable a network that is similar to the one in Figure 4-1.1. You can use any router that meets the interface requirements in Figure 4-1.1 (that is, 800, 1600, 1700, 2500, and 2600 routers or a combination). Refer to the information in Appendix C, "Router Interface Summary Chart," to correctly specify the interface identifiers based on the equipment in your lab. The 1721 series routers produced the configuration output in this lab. Another router might produce slightly different output. You should execute the following steps on each router unless you are specifically instructed otherwise. Start a HyperTerminal session.

Implement the procedure that is documented in Appendix A, "Erasing and Reloading the Router," on all routers before you continue with this lab.

Step 1. Configure the routers.

On the routers, enter the global configuration mode and configure the host name as shown in the chart. Then configure the console, virtual terminal, and enable passwords. Next, configure the interfaces according to the Lab Equipment Configuration tables. Finally, configure the IP host names. Do not configure the routing protocol until you are specifically told to. If you have problems configuring the router basics, refer to Lab 2-2, "Review of Basic Router Configuration with RIP (TI 1.2.3)."

Step 2. Save the configuration information from the privileged EXEC command mode.

```
Paris# copy running-config startup-config
Destination filename [startup-config]? [Enter]
```

Step 3. Configure the hosts with the proper IP address, subnet mask, and default gateway.

A. Each workstation should be able to **ping** the attached router. Troubleshoot as necessary. Hint: Remember to assign a specific IP address and default gateway to the workstation. If you are running Windows 98, check using **Start>Run>winipcfg**. If you are running Windows 2000, check using **ipconfig** in a DOS window.

B. At this point, the workstations will not be able to communicate with each other. The following steps demonstrate the process that is required to get communication working while using EIGRP as the routing protocol.

Step 4. View the router's configuration and interface information.

A. At the privileged EXEC mode prompt, type the following:

```
Paris#show running-config
```

B. Using the **show ip interface brief** command, check the status of each interface.

C. What is the state of the interfaces on each router?

Paris:

Fast Ethernet 0: _____

Serial 0: _____

Warsaw:

Fast Ethernet 0: _____

Serial 0: _____

D. **Ping** from one of the connected serial interfaces to the other.

E. Was the **ping** successful? _____

F. If the **ping** was not successful, troubleshoot the router's configuration until the **ping** is successful.

Step 5. Configure EIGRP routing on router Paris.

A. Enable the EIGRP routing process on Paris, and configure the networks it will advertise. Use EIGRP autonomous system number 101.

```
Paris(config)#router eigrp 101
Paris(config-router)#network 192.168.3.0
Paris(config-router)#network 192.168.2.0
Paris(config-router)#network 192.168.0.0
Paris(config-router)#end
```

B. Show the routing table for the Paris router.

```
Paris#show ip route
```

C.   Do entries exist in the routing table? _____

D.   Why?

_____

Step 6. Configure EIGRP routing on router Warsaw.

A.   Enable the EIGRP routing process on Warsaw, and configure the networks it will advertise. Use EIGRP autonomous system number 101.

```
Warsaw(config)#router eigrp 101
Warsaw(config-router)#network 192.168.2.0
Warsaw(config-router)#network 192.168.1.0
Warsaw(config-router)#end
```

B.   Show the routing table for the Warsaw router.

```
Warsaw#show ip route
```

Step 7. Test network connectivity.

Ping the Paris host from the Warsaw host. Was it successful? _____

If not, troubleshoot as necessary.

After you complete the previous steps, log off (by typing **exit**) and turn the router off. Then remove and store the cables and adapter.

Lab 4-2   Verifying Basic EIGRP Configuration (TI 3.2.3)

Figure 4-2-1 Topology for Lab 4-2

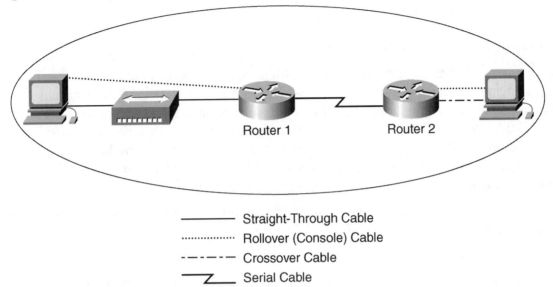

——————— Straight-Through Cable

················· Rollover (Console) Cable

— · — · — Crossover Cable

⎯z⎯ Serial Cable

Table 4-2-1   Lab Equipment Configuration: Part I

Router Designation	Router Name	Routing Protocol	Network Statements
Router 1	Paris	EIGRP	192.168.3.0 192.168.2.0
Router 2	Warsaw	EIGRP	192.168.1.0 192.168.2.0

The enable secret password for both routers is **class**.

The enable, VTY, and console password for both routers is **cisco**.

Table 4-2-2   Lab Equipment Configuration: Part II

Router Designation	Fast Ethernet 0 Address/ Subnet Mask	Interface Type Serial 0	Serial 0 Address/ Subnet Mask	Loopback 0 Address/ Subnet Mask	IP Host Table Entry
Router 1	192.168.3.1/24	DCE	192.168.2.1/30	192.168.0.2/24	Warsaw
Router 2	192.168.1.1/24	DTE	192.168.2.2/30	No Address	Paris

The IP Host Table Entry column contents indicate the names of the other routers in the IP host table.

Objectives

- Set up an IP addressing scheme for the network.
- Configure and verify EIGRP routing.

Background/Preparation

Cable a network that is similar to the one in Figure 4-2-1. You can use any router that meets the interface requirements in Figure 4-2-1 (that is, 800, 1600, 1700, 2500, and 2600 routers or a combination). Refer to the information in Appendix C to correctly specify the interface identifiers based on the equipment in your lab. The 1721 series routers produced the configuration output in this lab. Another router might produce slightly different output. You should execute the following steps on each router unless you are specifically instructed otherwise. Start a HyperTerminal session.

Implement the procedure documented in Appendix A on all routers before you continue with this lab.

Step 1. Configure the routers.

On the routers, enter the global configuration mode and configure the host name as shown in Tables 4-2-1 and 4-2-2. Then configure the console, virtual terminal, and enable passwords. Next, configure the interfaces according to Tables 4-2-1 and 4-2-2. Finally, configure the IP host names. Do not configure the routing protocol until you are specifically told to. If you have problems configuring the router basics, refer to Lab 2-2, "Review of Basic Router Configuration with RIP (TI 1.2.3)."

Step 2. Save the configuration information from the privileged EXEC command mode.

```
PARIS# copy running-config startup-config
Destination filename [startup-config]? [Enter]
```

Step 3. Configure the hosts with the proper IP address, subnet mask, and default gateway.

    A.   Each workstation should be able to ping the attached router. Troubleshoot as necessary. Hint: Remember to assign a specific IP address and default gateway to the workstation. If you are running Windows 98, check using **Start>Run>winipcfg**. If you are running Windows 2000, check using **ipconfig** in a DOS window.

    B.   At this point, the workstations will not be able to communicate with each other. The following steps demonstrate the process that is required to get communication working while using EIGRP as the routing protocol.

Step 4. View the router configuration and interface information.

    A.   At the privileged EXEC mode prompt, type the following:

```
Paris#show running-config
```

    B.   Using the **show ip interface brief** command, check the status of each interface.

C.   What is the state of the interfaces on each router?

Paris:

Fast Ethernet 0: _____

Serial 0: _____

Warsaw:

Fast Ethernet 0: _____

Serial 0: _____

D.   **Ping** from one of the connected serial interfaces to the other.

E.   Was the **ping** successful? _____

F.   If the **ping** was not successful, troubleshoot the router's configuration until the **ping** is successful.

Step 5. Configure EIGRP routing on router Paris.

A.   Enable the EIGRP routing process on Paris, and configure the networks it will advertise. Use EIGRP autonomous system number 101.

```
Paris(config)#router eigrp 101
Paris(config-router)#network 192.168.3.0
Paris(config-router)#network 192.168.2.0
Paris(config-router)#network 192.168.0.0
Paris(config-router)#end
```

B.   Show the routing table for the Paris router.

```
Paris#show ip route
```

C.   Do entries exist in the routing table? _____

D.   Why?

_____

Step 6. Configure EIGRP routing on router Warsaw.

A.   Enable the EIGRP routing process on Warsaw, and configure the networks it will advertise. Use EIGRP autonomous system number 101.

```
Warsaw(config)#router eigrp 101
Warsaw(config-router)#network 192.168.2.0
Warsaw(config-router)#network 192.168.1.0
Warsaw(config-router)#end
```

B.   Show the routing table for the Warsaw router.

```
Warsaw#show ip route
```

C.   Do EIGRP entries exist in the routing table now? _____

D.   What is the address type in the EIGRP 192.168.2.0 route?

_____

E.   What does the D mean in the first column of the routing table?

_____

Step 7. Show EIGRP neighbors.

A.   From the Paris router, show any neighbors that are connected by using the **show ip eigrp neighbors** command at the privileged EXEC mode prompt.

B.   Are neighbors shown? _____

Step 8. Test network connectivity.

A.   **Ping** the Paris host from the Warsaw host. Was it successful? _____

B.   If not, troubleshoot as necessary.

Step 9. View the topology table.

A.   To view the topology table, issue the **show ip eigrp topology all-links** command.

B.   How many routes are in passive mode? _____

C.   To view more specific information about a topology table entry, use an IP address with this command:

```
Paris#show ip eigrp topology 192.168.1.0
```

D.   Based on the output of this command, does it tell what external protocol originated this route to 192.168.2.0? _____

E.   Does it tell which router originated the route? _____

F.   Finally, use **show** commands to view key EIGRP statistics. On the Paris router, issue the **show ip eigrp traffic** command.

G.   How many hello packets has the Paris router received? _____

H.   How many has it sent? _____

After you complete the previous steps, log off (by typing **exit**) and turn the router off. Then remove and store the cables and adapter.

CCNA 3

Chapter 5: Switching Concepts and LAN Design

There are no hands-on labs associated with the topic of this chapter. Please review the information in Chapter 5 of the *Cisco Networking Academy Program CCNA 3 and 4 Companion Guide* to ensure that you can do the following:

- Describe Ethernet/802.3 LANs

- Understand LAN switching concepts

- Understand and utilize LAN design concepts

- Describe basic Layer 2 bridging and switching processes

CCNA 3

Chapter 6: Switches

There are no hands-on labs associated with the topic of this chapter. Please review the information in Chapter 6 of the *Cisco Networking Academy Program CCNA 3 and 4 Companion Guide* to ensure that you can do the following:

- Start a switch
- Identify the components of a switch
- Describe and identify where access layer switches are used
- Describe and identify where distribution layer switches are used
- Describe and identify where core layer switches are used

CCNA 3

Chapter 7: Switch Configuration

The following table maps the numbering scheme that is used in this chapter's labs to the Target Indicators (TIs) that are used in the online curriculum.

Lab Companion Numbering	Online Curriculum TI
Lab 7-1	6.2.1
Lab 7-2	6.2.2
Lab 7-3	6.2.3
Lab 7-4	6.2.4
Lab 7-5	6.2.5
Lab 7-6	6.2.6
Lab 7-7	6.2.7a
Lab 7-8	6.2.7b
Lab 7-9	6.2.8
Lab 7-10	6.2.9

Lab 7-1   Verifying Default Switch Configuration (TI 6.2.1)

Figure 7-1.1 Topology for Lab 7-1

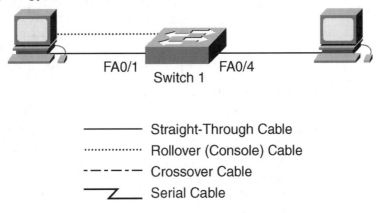

FA0/1   FA0/4
Switch 1

——————— Straight-Through Cable
·················· Rollover (Console) Cable
– – – – – Crossover Cable
⎯Z⎯ Serial Cable

Objective

Investigate the default configuration of a 2900 series switch.

Background/Preparation

Cable a network that is similar to the one in Figure 7-1.1. The 2950 series switch produced the configuration output in this lab. Another switch might produce different output. You should execute the following steps on each switch unless you are specifically instructed otherwise. Instructions are also provide for the 1900 Series switch, which initially displays a User Interface Menu. Select the **Command Line** option from the menu to perform the steps for this lab.

Start a HyperTerminal session.

Implement the procedure documented in Appendix B, "Erasing and Reloading the Switch," on all switches before you continue with this lab.

General Configuration Tips

- Use the question mark (?) and arrow keys help to enter commands.

- Each command mode restricts the set of available commands. If you have difficulty entering a command, check the prompt and then enter the question mark (**?**) for a list of available commands. You might be using the wrong command mode or the wrong syntax.

- To disable a feature, enter the keyword **no** before the command, such as **no ip address**.

- Save the configuration changes to NVRAM so that you do not lose the changes if there is a system reload or power outage.

- Table 7-1.2 shows the switch command modes that you should be familiar with for all labs in this chapter.

Table 7-1.2   *Switch Command Modes*

Command Mode	Access Method	Switch Prompt Displayed	Exit Method
User EXEC	Log in.	Switch>	Use the **logout** command.
Privileged EXEC	From user EXEC mode, enter the **enable** command.	Switch#	To exit to user EXEC mode, use the **disable**, **exit**, or **logout** commands.
Global Configuration	From the privileged EXEC mode, enter the **configure terminal** command.	Switch (config)#	To exit to privileged EXEC mode, use the **exit** or **end** command, or press **Ctrl+Z**.

Command Mode	Access Method	Switch Prompt Displayed	Exit Method
Interface Configuration	From the global configuration mode, enter the **interface** *type number* command, such as **interface serial 0**.	Switch (config-if)#	To exit to global configuration mode, use the **exit** command.

Step 1. Enter privileged mode.

    A.   Privileged mode gives access to all the switch commands. Because many of the privileged commands configure operating parameters, privileged access should be password-protected to prevent unauthorized use. The privileged command set includes those commands that are contained in user EXEC mode, as well as the **configure** command through which access to the remaining command modes is gained.

```
Switch>enable
Switch#
```

    B.   Notice that the prompt changed to reflect privileged EXEC mode.

Step 2. Examine the current switch configuration (1900: perform A, B, and K).

    A.   Examine the current running configuration file:

```
Switch#show running-config
```

    B.   How many Ethernet and/or Fast Ethernet interfaces does the switch have?

    _____

    C.   What is the range of values shown for the VTY lines?

    _____

    D.   Examine the current contents of NVRAM:

```
Switch#show startup-config

%% Non-volatile configuration memory is not present
```

    E.   Why does the switch give this response?

    _____

    _____

    F.   Show the current IP address of the switch.

```
Switch#show interface VLAN 1
```

    G.   Is an IP address set on the switch?

    H.   What is the MAC address of this virtual switch interface? _____

    I.   Is this interface up? _____

J.   You can show the IP properties of the interface by entering the following command:

```
Switch#show ip interface VLAN 1
```

K.   The following commands will provide the switch IP address information for the 1900:

```
#show ip
```

Step 3. Display Cisco IOS Software information.

A.   Examine the version information that the switch reports.

```
Switch#show version
```

B.   What is the IOS version that the switch is running? _____

C.   What is the system image filename? _____

D.   What is the base MAC address of this switch? _____

E.   Is the switch running Enhanced Image software? _____

Step 4. Examine the Fast Ethernet interfaces.

A.   Examine the default properties of the Fast Ethernet interfaces. As an example, examine the properties of the fourth interface:

```
Switch#show interface fastethernet 0/4 (Note: this can be a trunk
or access port)
Switch#show interface gigabitethernet 0/1 (Note: this can be a
trunk or access port)
```

1900:

```
Switch#show interface fastethernet 0/26 (Note: this is a trunk
port)
```

or

```
Switch#show interface ethernet 0/4 (Note: this is an access port)
```

B.   Is the interface up or down? _____

C.   What event would make an interface go up? _____

D.   What is the MAC address of the interface? _____

E.   What is the speed and duplex setting of the interface? _____

Step 5. Examine VLAN information.

A.   Examine the default VLAN settings of the switch.

```
Switch#show vlan
```

B.   What is the name of VLAN 1? _____

C.   Which ports are in this VLAN? _____

      D.   Is VLAN 1 active? _____

      E.   What type of VLAN is the default VLAN? _____

Step 6. Examine Flash memory (1900: skip to Step 8).

      A.   Examine the contents of the Flash directory:

```
Switch#dir flash:
```

or

```
Switch#show flash
```

      B.   Name the files and directories found.

                _____ _____

                _____

                _____

Step 7. Examine the startup configuration file.

      A.   To see the contents of the startup configuration file, type the **show startup-config** command in privileged EXEC mode.

```
Switch#show startup-config
```

      B.   The switch responds with the following:

```
Non-volatile configuration memory is not present
```

      C.   Why does this message appear?

                _____

      D.   Copy the current configuration to NVRAM. This step ensures that any changes made will be available to the switch if there is a reload or if the power goes off.

```
Switch#copy running-config startup-config
Destination filename [startup-config]?
Building configuration...
[OK]
Switch#
```

      E.   Show the contents of NVRAM:

```
Switch#show startup-config
```

      F.   What is displayed now? _____

Step 8. Exit the switch.

Exit to the switch welcome screen.

```
Switch#exit
```

After you complete the previous steps, log off (by typing **exit**) and turn all the devices off. Then remove and store the cables and adapter.

Lab 7-2   Basic Switch Configuration (TI 6.2.2)

Figure 7-2.1 Topology for Lab 7-2

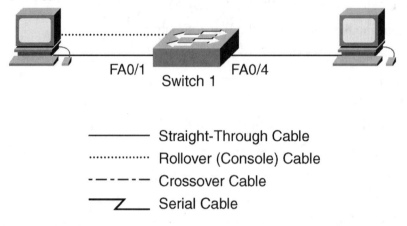

FA0/1   FA0/4
Switch 1

—————— Straight-Through Cable

················ Rollover (Console) Cable

— — — — — Crossover Cable

————Z—— Serial Cable

Table 7-2.1   Lab Equipment Configuration

Switch Designation	Switch Name	Enable Secret Password	Enable/VTY/Console Password
Switch 1	ALSwitch	**class**	**Cisco**

Objectives

- Configure a switch with a name and an IP address.
- Configure passwords to ensure that access to the CLI is secured.
- Configure switch port speed and duplex properties for an interface.
- Save the active configuration.
- View the switch browser interface.

Background/Preparation

Cable a network that is similar to the one in Figure 7-2.1. The 2950 series switch produced the configuration output used in this lab. Another switch might produce different output. You should execute the following steps on each switch unless you are specifically instructed otherwise. Instructions are also provided for the 1900 Series switch, which initially displays a User Interface Menu. Select the **Command Line** option from the menu to perform the steps for this lab.

Start a HyperTerminal session.

Implement the procedure documented in Appendix B, "Erasing and Reloading the Switch," before you continue with this lab.

Step 1. Enter privileged mode.

    A.   Privileged mode gives access to all the switch commands. Because many of the privileged commands configure operating parameters, privileged access should be password-protected to prevent unauthorized use. The privileged command set includes those commands that are contained in user EXEC mode, as well as the configure command through which access to the remaining command modes is gained.

```
Switch>enable
Switch#
```

1900:

```
>enable
#
```

    B.   Notice that the prompt changed to reflect privileged EXEC mode.

Step 2. Examine the current switch configuration.

    A.   Examine the current running configuration file.

```
Switch#show running-config
```

    B.   How many Ethernet or Fast Ethernet interfaces does the switch have? _____

    C.   What is the range of values shown for the VTY lines? _____

    D.   Examine the current contents of NVRAM:

```
Switch#show startup-config
%% Non-volatile configuration memory is not present
```

    E.   Why does the switch give this response?

_____

Step 3. Assign a name to the switch.

    A.   Enter enable and then configuration mode. Configuration mode allows the management of the switch. Enter the name by which this switch will be referred: ALSwitch

```
Switch#configure terminal
Enter configuration commands, one per line. End with Ctrl+Z.
Switch(config)#hostname ALSwitch
ALSwitch(config)#exit
```

    B.   Notice that the prompt changed to reflect its new name. Type **exit** or press **Ctrl+Z** to go back into privileged mode.

Step 4. Examine the current running configuration.

    A.   Examine the current configuration to verify that there is no configuration except for the host name.

```
ALSwitch#show running-config
```

B.   Are passwords set on lines? _____

C.   What does the configuration show as the host name of this switch?
        _____

Step 5. Set the access passwords (1900: skip to Step 6).

Enter config-line mode for the console. Set the password on this line to **cisco** for login.
Configure the VTY lines 0 to 15 with the password **cisco**:

```
ALSwitch#configure terminal
Enter configuration commands, one per line. End with Ctrl+Z.
ALSwitch(config)#line con 0
ALSwitch(config-line)#password cisco
ALSwitch(config-line)#login

ALSwitch(config-line)#line vty 0 15
ALSwitch(config-line)#password cisco
ALSwitch(config-line)#login

ALSwitch(config-line)#exit
```

Step 6. Set the command mode passwords.

A.   Set the enable password to **cisco** and the enable secret password to **class**.

```
ALSwitch(config)#enable password cisco

ALSwitch(config)#enable secret class
```

1900:
```
ALSwitch(config)#enable password level 15 cisco

ALSwitch(config)#enable secret class
```

B.   Which password takes precedence: the enable password or the enable secret
        password? _____

Step 7. Configure Layer 3 access to the switch.

A.   Set the IP address of the switch to 192.168.1.2 with a subnet mask of
        255.255.255.0. Note that this is done on the internal virtual interface VLAN 1.

```
ALSwitch(config)#interface VLAN 1
ALSwitch(config-if)#ip address 192.168.1.2 255.255.255.0
ALSwitch(config-if)#exit
```

1900:

```
ALSwitch(config)#ip address 192.168.1.2 255.255.255.0
ALSwitch(config)#exit
```

B. Set the default gateway for the switch and the default management VLAN as 192.168.1.1.

```
ALSwitch(config)#ip default-gateway 192.168.1.1
ALSwitch(config)#exit
```

1900:

```
ALSwitch(config)#ip default-gateway 192.168.1.1
ALSwitch(config)#exit
```

Step 8. Verify the management LAN settings (1900: skip to Step 9).

A. Verify the interface settings on VLAN 1.

```
ALSwitch#show interface VLAN 1
```

B. What is the bandwidth on this interface? _____

C. What are the VLAN states? VLAN1 is _____, and Line protocol is _____.

D. Enable the virtual interface using the **no shutdown** command

```
ALSwitch(config)#interface VLAN 1
```

```
ALSwitch(config-if)#no shutdown
```

```
ALSwitch(config-if)#exit
```

E. What is the queuing strategy? _____

Step 9. Configure port speed and duplex properties for a Fast Ethernet interface.

(Note: 1900 switch access ports can only operate at 10 Mbps, but duplex can be set to full. If the switch has 10/100 Mbps trunk ports, the speed and duplex can be set for these.)

Prepare to configure the interface fastethernet 0/4 interface.

```
ALSwitch#configure terminal
```

Enter configuration commands, one per line. End with **Ctrl+Z**.

```
ALSwitch(config)#interface fastethernet 0/4
```

A. Set the port speed of interface fastethernet 0/4 to 100 Mbps and to operate in full-duplex mode.

```
ALSwitch(config-if)#speed 100
ALSwitch(config-if)#duplex full
```

B. If you know that the devices that are connected to a port must operate at a certain speed and in duplex mode, you should set the interface to that speed and mode.

Step 10. Verify the settings on a Fast Ethernet interface.

```
ALSwitch#show interface fastethernet 0/4
```

Step 11. Save the configuration.

The basic configuration of the switch has just been completed. Back up the running configuration file to NVRAM. This ensures that the changes made will not be lost if the system is rebooted or loses power.

```
ALSwitch#copy running-config startup-config
Destination filename [startup-config]?[Enter]
Building configuration...
[OK]
ALSwitch#
```

1900:

The configuration is automatically saved to NVRAM within approximately one minute of entering a command. To save the configuration to a TFTP server, enter the following

```
ALSwitch#copy nvram tftp://tftp server ip address/destination_filename
```

Step 12. Examine the startup configuration file (1900: skip to Step 13).

A. To see the configuration that is stored in NVRAM, type **show startup-config** from the privileged EXEC (enable) mode.

```
ALSwitch#show startup-config
```

B. What is displayed? _____

C. Are all the changes that were entered recorded in the file? _____

Step 13. Remove the enable password and the enable secret password.

```
ALSwitch#configure terminal
Enter configuration commands, one per line.  End with Ctrl+Z.
ALSwitch(config)#no enable password
ALSwitch(config)#no enable secret
```

1900:

```
ALSwitch(config)#no enable password level 15
ALSwitch(config)#no enable secret
```

Step 14. Access the switch web interface.

A. Access to the web interface of the switch may be on by default. If it is not on, issue the following command:

```
ALSwitch(config)#ip http server
```

B. Verify that your PC has an IP address and subnet mask that is compatible with the switch VLAN 1 IP address. Start your web browser.

C. Type the switch IP address into the **Location** field (Netscape) or **Address** field (Internet Explorer) and press **Enter**.

D. Because you have not secured access to the switch web interface, you will get a web page from the switch. You will not be asked to supply a username or password.

E. What are the names of the active links?

_____

_____

_____

Step 15. Exit the switch.

Exit to the switch welcome screen.

```
ALSwitch#exit
```

After you complete the previous steps, log off (by typing **exit**) and turn all the devices off. Then remove and store the cables and adapter.

Lab 7-3   Managing the MAC Address Table (TI 6.2.3)

Figure 7-3.1 Topology for Lab 7-3

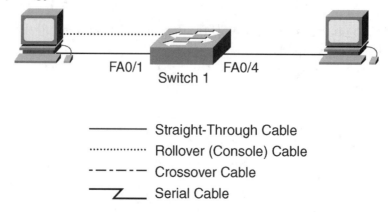

———— Straight-Through Cable

.... Rollover (Console) Cable

– – – – – Crossover Cable

———ϟ— Serial Cable

Table 7-3.1   Lab Equipment Configuration

Switch Designation	Switch Name	VLAN 1 IP Address	Default Gateway IP Address	Subnet Mask
Switch 1	ALSwitch	192.168.1.2	192.168.1.1	255.255.255.0

The enable secret password is **class**.

The enable, VTY, and console password is **cisco**.

Objective

Create a basic switch configuration and manage the switch MAC table.

Background/Preparation

Cable a network that is similar to the one in Figure 7-3.1. The 2950 switch produced the configuration output in this lab. Another switch might produce different output. Instructions are also provided for the 1900 Series switch, which initially displays a User Interface Menu. Select the **Command Line** option from the menu to perform the steps for this lab.

Start a HyperTerminal session.

Implement the procedure documented in Appendix B, "Erasing and Reloading the Switch," on all switches before you continue with this lab.

Step 1. Configure the switch.

Configure the host name and passwords, as well as the management VLAN 1 settings for the switch, as indicated in Table 7-3.1. If you have problems while performing this configuration, refer to Lab 7-2, "Basic Switch Configuration (TI 6.2.2)."

Step 2. Configure the hosts that are attached to the switch.

Configure the hosts to use the same IP subnet for addresses, masks, and the default gateway as the switch.

Step 3. Verify connectivity.

    A.   To verify that the hosts and switch are correctly configured, **ping** the switch IP address from the hosts.

    B.   Were the **ping**s successful? _____

    C.   If the answer is no, troubleshoot the hosts and switch configurations.

Step 4. Record the host MAC addresses.

    A.   Determine and record the Layer 2 addresses of the PC network interface cards.

          If you are running Windows 98, check using **Start>Run>winipcfg**. Click on **More info**.

          If you are running Windows 2000, check using **Start>Run>cmd>ipconfig /all**.

    B.   PC1: _____

    C.   PC4: _____

Step 5. Determine the MAC addresses that the switch has learned.

    A.   Determine the MAC addresses that the switch has learned by using the **show mac-address-table** command at the privileged EXEC mode prompt.

```
ALSwitch#show mac-address-table
```

    B.   How many dynamic addresses exist? _____

    C.   How many MAC addresses exist? _____

    D.   How many addresses have been user defined? _____

    E.   Do the MAC addresses match the host MAC addresses? _____

Step 6. Determine the **show mac-address-table** options.

    A.   Determine the options that the **show mac-address-table** command has by using the **?** option.

```
ALSwitch#show mac-address-table ?
```

    B.   How many options are available for the **show mac-address-table** command? _____

    C.   Show only the MAC addresses from the table that were learned dynamically.

    D.   How many exist? _____

Step 7. Clear the MAC address table.

Remove the existing MAC addresses by using the clear mac-address-table command from the privileged EXEC mode prompt.

```
ALSwitch#clear mac-address-table dynamic
```

Step 8. Verify the results.

    A.   Verify that the **mac-address-table** was cleared.

          `ALSwitch#`**`show mac-address-table`**

    B.   How many MAC addresses exist now? _____

    C.   How many dynamic addresses exist? _____

Step 9. Determine the **clear mac-address-table** command options.

    A.   Determine the options that are available with the command **clear mac-address-table ?** at the privileged EXEC mode prompt.

          `ALSwitch#`**`clear mac-address-table ?`**

    B.   How many options exist? _____

    C.   In what circumstances would these options be used?

          _____

Step 10. Examine the MAC table again.

    A.   Look at the MAC address table again by using the **show mac-address-table** command at the privileged EXEC mode prompt.

          `ALSwitch#`**`show mac-address-table`**

    B.   How many dynamic addresses exist? _____

    C.   Why did this change from the last display?

          _____

    D.   If the table has not changed yet, **ping** the switch IP address from the hosts two times each and repeat step 10.

Step 11. Exit the switch.

Exit to the switch welcome screen.

          `Switch#`**`exit`**

After you complete the previous steps, log off (by typing **exit**) and turn all the devices off. Then remove and store the cables and adapter.

Lab 7-4   Configuring Static MAC Addresses (TI 6.2.4)

Figure 7-4.1 Topology for Lab 7-4

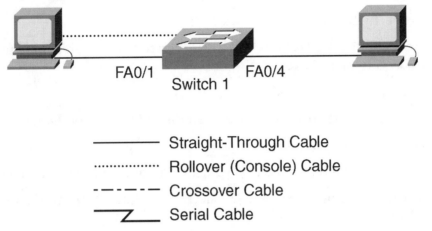

FA0/1

Switch 1

FA0/4

——————— Straight-Through Cable

················· Rollover (Console) Cable

– – – – – Crossover Cable

⎯⎯Z⎯⎯ Serial Cable

Table 7-4.1 Lab Equipment Configuration

Switch Designation	Switch Name	VLAN 1 IP Address	Default Gateway IP Address	Subnet Mask
Switch 1	ALSwitch	192.168.1.2	192.168.1.1	255.255.255.0

The enable secret password is **class**.

The enable, VTY, and console password is **cisco**.

Objectives

- Create a static address entry in the switch MAC table.

- Remove the created static MAC address entry.

Background/Preparation

Cable a network that is similar to the one in Figure 7-4.1. The 2950 switch produced the configuration output in this lab. Another switch might produce different output. Instructions are also provided for the 1900 Series switch, which initially displays a User Interface Menu. Select the **Command Line** option from the menu to perform the steps for this lab.

Start a HyperTerminal session.

Implement the procedure documented in Appendix B, "Erasing and Reloading the Switch," on all switches before you continue with this lab.

Step 1. Configure the switch.

Configure the host name and passwords as well as the management VLAN 1 settings for the switch, as indicated in Table 7-4.1. If you have problems while performing this configuration, refer to Lab 7-2, "Basic Switch Configuration (TI 6.2.2)."

Step 2. Configure the hosts that are attached to the switch.

Configure the hosts to use the same IP subnet for addresses, masks, and the default gateway as the switch.

Step 3. Verify connectivity.

A.   To verify that the hosts and switch are correctly configured, **ping** the switch IP address from the hosts.

B.   Were the **ping**s successful? _____

C.   If the answer is no, troubleshoot the hosts and switch configurations.

Step 4. Record the host MAC addresses.

A.   Determine and record the Layer 2 addresses of the PC network interface cards.

If you are running Windows 98, check using **Start>Run>winipcfg**. Click on **More info**.

If you are running Windows 2000, check using **Start>Run>cmd>ipconfig /all**.

B.   PC1: _____

C.   PC4: _____

Step 5. Determine the MAC addresses that the switch has learned.

A.   Determine the MAC addresses that the switch has learned by using the **show mac-address-table** command at the privileged EXEC mode prompt.

```
ALSwitch#show mac-address-table
```

B.   How many dynamic addresses exist? _____

C.   How many MAC addresses exist? _____

D.   Do the MAC addresses match the host MAC addresses? _____

Step 6. Determine the **show mac-address-table** options.

A.   Determine the options that the **mac-address-table** command has using the **?** option.

```
ALSwitch(config)#mac-address-table ?
```

B.   How many options are available for the **mac-address-table** command?

_____

C.   There is an option to set a static MAC address in the table. Under what circumstances would you utilize this option?

_____

Step 7. Set up a static MAC address.

Set up a static MAC address on Fast Ethernet interface 0/4. Use the address that was recorded for PC4 in Step 4. The MAC address 00e0.2917.1884 is used in the example statement only.

```
ALSwitch(config)#mac-address-table static 00e0.2917.1884 interface
fastethernet 0/4 vlan 1
```

1900:

```
ALSwitch(config)#mac-address-table permanent 00e0.2917.1884 ethernet 0/4
```

Step 8. Verify the results.

A.   Verify the MAC address table entries.

```
ALSwitch#show mac-address-table
```

B.   How many MAC addresses exist now? _____

C.   How many static addresses exist? _____

D.   Under what circumstances can other static or dynamic learning of addresses occur on switchport 4?

_____

Step 9. Remove the static MAC entry.

You might need to reverse the **static mac-address-table** entry. To do this, enter the configuration mode and reverse the command by putting a **no** in front the entire old command string. The MAC address 00e0.2917.1884 is used in the example statement only. Use the MAC address that was recorded for the host on port 0/4.

```
ALSwitch(config)#no mac-address-table static 00e0.2917.1884 interface
    fastethernet 0/4 vlan 1
```

1900:

```
ALSwitch(config)#no mac-address-table permanent 00e0.2917.1884
    ethernet 0/4
```

Step 10. Verify the results.

A.   Verify that the static MAC address was cleared.

```
ALSwitch#show mac-address-table static
```

B.   How many static MAC addresses exist now? _____

Step 11. Exit the switch.

Exit to the switch welcome screen.

```
Switch#exit
```

After you complete the previous steps, log off (by typing **exit**) and turn all the devices off. Then remove and store the cables and adapter.

Lab 7-5   Configuring Port Security (TI 6.2.5)

Figure 7-5.1 Topology for Lab 7-5

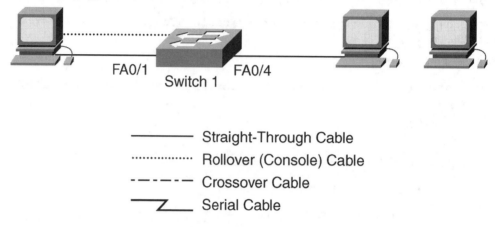

FA0/1   FA0/4
Switch 1

——————— Straight-Through Cable

················· Rollover (Console) Cable

– – – – – – Crossover Cable

——⌐Z—— Serial Cable

Table 7-5.1   Lab Equipment Configuration

Switch Designation	Switch Name	VLAN 1 IP Address	Default Gateway IP Address	Subnet Mask
Switch 1	ALSwitch	192.168.1.2	192.168.1.1	255.255.255.0

The enable secret password is **class**.

The enable, VTY, and console password is **cisco**.

Objectives

- Create and verify a basic switch configuration.

- Configure port security on individual Fast Ethernet ports.

Background/Preparation

Cable a network that is similar to the one in Figure 7-5.1. The 2950 switch produced the configuration output in this lab. Another switch might produce different output. Instructions are also provided for the 1900 Series switch, which initially displays a User Interface Menu. Select the **Command Line** option from the menu to perform the steps for this lab.

Start a HyperTerminal session.

Implement the procedure documented in Appendix B, "Erasing and Reloading the Switch," on all switches before you continue with this lab.

Step 1. Configure the switch.

Configure the host name and passwords, as well as the management VLAN 1 settings for the switch, as indicated in Table 7-5.1. If you have problems while performing this configuration, refer to Lab 7-2, "Basic Switch Configuration (TI 6.2.2)."

Step 2. Configure the hosts that are attached to the switch.

A.   Configure the hosts to use the same IP subnet for addresses, masks, and the default gateway as the switch.

B.   You need a third host for this lab. You must configure this host with the address 192.168.1.7. The subnet mask is 255.255.255.0 and the default gateway is 192.168.1.1. Do *not* connect this PC to the switch yet.

Step 3. Verify connectivity.

A.   To verify that the hosts and switch are configured correctly, **ping** the switch IP address from the hosts.

B.   Were the **ping**s successful? _____

C.   If the answer is no, troubleshoot the hosts and switch configurations.

Step 4. Record the hosts' MAC addresses.

A.   Determine and record the layer 2 addresses of the PC network interface cards.

If you are running Windows 98, check using **Start>Run>winipcfg**. Click on **More info**.

If you are running Windows 2000, check using **Start>Run>cmd>ipconfig /all**.

B.   PC1: _____

C.   PC4: _____

Step 5. Determine the MAC addresses that the switch has learned.

A.   Determine the MAC addresses that the switch has learned by using the **show mac-address-table** command at the privileged EXEC mode prompt.

```
ALSwitch#show mac-address-table
```

B.   How many dynamic addresses exist? _____

C.   How many MAC addresses exist? _____

D.   Do the MAC addresses match the host MAC addresses? _____

Step 6. Determine the **show mac-address-table** options.

Determine the options that the **mac-address-table** command has using the **?** option.

```
ALSwitch(config)#mac-address-table ?
```

Step 7. Set up a static MAC address.

Set up a static MAC address on Fast Ethernet interface 0/4. Use the address that was recorded for PC4 in Step 4. The MAC address 00e0.2917.1884 is used in the example statement only.

```
ALSwitch(config)#mac-address-table static 00e0.2917.1884 interface
    fastethernet 0/4 vlan 1
```

1900:

```
ALSwitch(config)#mac-address-table permanent 00e0.2917.1884 ethernet
    0/4
```

Step 8. Verify the results.

    A.   Verify the MAC address table entries.

```
ALSwitch#show mac-address-table
```

    B.   How many static addresses exist? _____

Step 9. List port security options.

    A.   Determine options for setting port security on interface Fast Ethernet 0/4.

```
ALSwitch(config)#interface fastethernet 0/4

ALSwitch(config-if)#switchport port-security   ?
  aging        Port-security aging commands
  mac-address  Secure mac address
  maximum      Max secure addrs
  violation    Security Violation Mode
  <cr>
```

        1900:

```
ALSwitch(config)#interface ethernet 0/4
ALSwitch(config-if)#port secure ?
  max-mac-count  Maximum number of addresses allowed on the port
  <cr>
```

    B.   Allow the switchport fastethernet 0/4 to accept only one device:

```
ALSwitch(config-if)#switchport mode access
ALSwitch(config-if)#switchport port-security
ALSwitch(config-if)#switchport port-security mac-address 1
```

        1900:

```
ALSwitch(config-if)#port secure
```

        2900:

```
ALSwitch(config-if)#port security
```

Step 10. Verify the results.

    A.   Verify the MAC address table entries.

```
ALSwitch#show mac-address-table
```

    B.   How are the address types listed for the two MAC addresses? _____

    C.   Show port security settings

```
ALSwitch#show port-security interface fastethernet 0/4
```

        1900:

```
ALSwitch#show mac-address-table security
```

Step 11. Show the running configuration file.

A.   Do some statements directly reflect the security implementation in the listing of the running configuration? _____

B.   What do those statements mean?

_____

_____

_____

Step 12. Limit the number of hosts per port.

A.   On interface fastethernet 0/4, set the port security maximum MAC count to 1.

```
ALSwitch(config)#interface fastethernet 0/4
ALSwitch(config-if)#switchport port-security maximum 1
```

1900:

```
ALSwitch(config)#interface Ethernet 0/4
ALSwitch(config-if)#port secure max-mac-count 1
```

B.   Disconnect the PC that is attached to fastethernet 0/4 and connect to that port the PC that has been given the IP address 192.168.1.7. This PC has not been attached to the switch. To generate some traffic, you might need to **ping** the switch address 192.168.1.2.

C.   Record your observations.

_____

_____

_____

Step 13. Configure the port to shut down if a security violation occurs.

A.   If a security violation occurs, you should shut down the interface. Make the port security action shut down.

```
ALSwitch(config-if)#switchport port-security violation shutdown
```

2900XL:

```
ALSwitch(config-if)#port security action shutdown
```

1900:

```
The default action upon address violation is "suspend"
```

B.   What other action options are available with port security?

_____

C.   If necessary, **ping** the switch address 192.168.1.2 from the PC 192.168.1.7 that is now connected to interface fastethernet 0/4. This ensures that there is traffic from the PC to the switch.

D.   Record your observations.

_____

_____

_____

Step 14. Show port 0/4 configuration information.

A.   To see the configuration information for Fast Ethernet port 0/4, type **show interface fastethernet 0/4** at the privileged EXEC mode prompt.

```
ALSwitch#show interface fastethernet 0/4
```

1900:

```
ALSwitch#show interface ethernet 0/4
```

B.   What is the state of this interface?

C.   Fast Ethernet 0/4 is _____, and line protocol is _____.

Step 15. Reactivate the port.

A.   If a security violation occurs and the port is shut down, use the **no shutdown** command to reactivate it.

B.   Try this a few times switching between the original port 0/4 host and the new one. Plug in the original host, type the **no shutdown** command on the interface, and **ping** by using the DOS window. You have to repeat the **ping** multiple times or use the **ping 192.168.1.2 -n 200** command. This sets the number of ping packets to 200 instead of 4. Then switch hosts and try again.

Step 16. Exit the switch.

Exit to the switch welcome screen.

```
Switch#exit
```

After you complete the previous steps, log off (by typing **exit**) and turn all the devices off. Then remove and store the cables and adapter.

Lab 7-6   Add, Move, and Change MAC Addresses (TI 6.2.6)

Figure 7-6.1   Topology for Lab 7-6

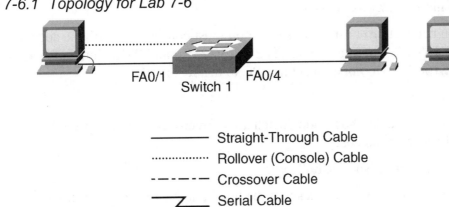

FA0/1   FA0/4

Switch 1

——————— Straight-Through Cable

·················· Rollover (Console) Cable

– – – – – Crossover Cable

⎯⎯⎯⎯Z⎯⎯⎯ Serial Cable

Table 7-6.1   Lab Equipment Configuration

Switch Designation	Switch Name	VLAN 1 IP Address	Default Gateway IP Address	Subnet Mask
Switch 1	ALSwitch	192.168.1.2	192.168.1.1	255.255.255.0

The enable secret password is **class**.

The enable, VTY, and console password is **cisco**.

Objectives

- Create and verify a basic switch configuration.

- Move a PC from one switch port to another and add a new PC to the switch.

Background/Preparation

Cable a network that is similar to the one in Figure 7-6.1. The 2950 switch produced the configuration output in this lab. Another switch might produce different output. Instructions are also provided for the 1900 Series switch, which initially displays a User Interface Menu. Select the **Command Line** option from the menu to perform the steps for this lab.

Start a HyperTerminal session.

Implement the procedure documented in Appendix B, "Erasing and Reloading the Switch," before you continue with this lab.

Step 1. Configure the switch.

Configure the host name and passwords, as well as the management VLAN 1 settings for the switch, as indicated in Table 7-6.1. If you have problems while performing this configuration, refer to Lab 7-2, "Basic Switch Configuration (TI 6.2.2)."

Step 2. Configure the hosts that are attached to the switch.

    A.   Configure the hosts to use the same IP subnet for addresses, masks, and the default gateway as the switch.

    B.   You need a third host for this lab. You must configure it with the address 192.168.1.7. The subnet mask is 255.255.255.0 and the default gateway is 192.168.1.1. Do *not* connect this PC to the switch yet.

Step 3. Verify connectivity.

    A.   To verify that the hosts and switch are correctly configured, **ping** the switch IP address from the hosts.

    B.   Were the **ping**s successful? _____

    C.   If the answer is no, troubleshoot the hosts and switch configurations.

Step 4. Record the hosts' MAC addresses.

    A.   Determine and record the Layer 2 addresses of the PC network interface cards.

        If you are running Windows 98, check using **Start>Run>winipcfg**. Click on **More info**.

        If you are running Windows 2000, check using **Start>Run>cmd>ipconfig /all**.

    B.   PC1: _____

    C.   PC4: _____

Step 5. Determine the MAC addresses that the switch has learned.

    A.   Determine the MAC addresses that the switch has learned by using the **show mac-address-table** command at the privileged EXEC mode prompt.

```
ALSwitch#show mac-address-table
```

    B.   How many dynamic addresses exist? _____

    C.   How many MAC addresses exist? _____

    D.   Do the MAC addresses match the host MAC addresses? _____

Step 6. Determine the **show mac-address-table** command options.

Determine the options that the **mac-address-table** command has using the **?** option.

```
ALSwitch(config)#mac-address-table ?
```

Step 7. Set up a static MAC address.

Set up a static MAC address on Fast Ethernet interface 0/4. Use the address that was recorded for PC4 in Step 4. The MAC address 00e0.2917.1884 is used in the example statement only.

```
ALSwitch(config)#mac-address-table static 00e0.2917.1884 vlan 1
interface fastethernet 0/4
```

1900:

```
ALSwitch(config)#mac-address-table permanent 00e0.2917.1884 ethernet
   0/4
```

Step 8. Verify the results.

A.   Verify the mac address table entries.

```
ALSwitch#show mac-address-table
```

B.   How many static addresses exist? _____

Step 9. List port security options.

A.   Determine options for setting port security on interface Fast Ethernet 0/4. Type
port security ? from the interface configuration prompt for Fast Ethernet port
0/4.

```
ALSwitch(config)#interface fastethernet 0/4
ALSwitch(config-if)#port security ?
  aging          Port-security aging commands
  mac-address    Secure mac address
  maximum        Max secure addrs
  violation      Security Violation Mode
  <cr>
```

1900:

```
ALSwitch(config)#interface ethernet 0/4
ALSwitch(config-if)#port secure ?
  max-mac-count  Maximum number of addresses allowed on the port
  <cr>
```

B.   Allow the switchport Fast Ethernet 0/4 to accept only one device by typing **port
security**.

```
ALSwitch(config-if)#switchport mode access
ALSwitch(config-if)#switchport port-security
ALSwitch(config-if)#switchport port-security mac-address sticky
```

1900:

```
ALSwitch(config-if)#port secure
```

Step 10. Verify the results.

A.   Verify the MAC address table entries.

```
ALSwitch#show mac-address-table
```

B.   How are the address types listed for the two MAC addresses? _____

Step 11. Show the running configuration file.

    A.   In the listing of the running configuration, do some statements directly reflect the security implementation? _____

    B.   What do those statements mean?

_____

_____

_____

Step 12. Limit the number of hosts per port.

    A.   On interface Fast Ethernet 0/4, set the port security maximum MAC count to 1.

```
ALSwitch(config)#interface fastethernet 0/4
ALSwitch(config-if)#switchport port-security maximum 1
```

1900:

```
ALSwitch(config)#interface ethernet 0/4
ALSwitch(config-if)#port secure max-mac-count 1
```

    B.   Disconnect the PC that is attached to Fast Ethernet 0/4 and connect to that port the PC that has been given the IP address 192.168.1.7. This PC has not been attached to the switch. To generate some traffic, **ping** the switch address 192.168.1.2 with the **-n 50** option. For example, use **ping 192.168.1.2 -n 50**, where 50 is the number of **ping**s sent.

Step 13. Move host.

    A.   Reconnect the PC that had previously been connected to Fast Ethernet 0/4 to Fast Ethernet 0/8. The PC has been moved to a new location. This could be to another VLAN, but in this instance, all switch ports are in VLAN 1 and network 192.168.1.0.

    B.   From this PC on Fast Ethernet 0/8, **ping 192.168.1.2 -n 50**.

    C.   Was this successful? _____

    D.   Why or why not?

_____

    E.   Show the MAC address table.

```
ALSwitch#show mac-address-table
```

    F.   Record observations about the show output.

_____

_____

_____

Step 14. Clear the MAC address table.

    A.   Clear the MAC address table. Doing so unlocks the MAC addresses from security and allows a new address to be registered.

```
ALSwitch#clear mac-address-table dynamic
```

    B.   From the PC on the Fast Ethernet 0/8, **ping 192.168.1.2 -n 50**.

C.   Was this successful? _____

D.   If not, troubleshoot as necessary.

Step 15. Change the security settings.

A.   Show the MAC address table.

```
ALSwitch#show mac-address-table
```

B.   Observe that Fast Ethernet 0/4 is secure but that the security should be applied to the machine on port 0/8 because this is the machine that was moved form port 0/4. Remove port security from interface Fast Ethernet 0/4.

```
ALSwitch(config)#interface fastethernet 0/4
ALSwitch(config-if)#no switchport port-security
ALSwitch(config-if)#no switchport port-security mac-address
  sticky
ALSwitch(config-if)#shutdown
ALSwitch(config-if)#no shutdown
```

1900:

```
ALSwitch(config)#interface ethernet 0/4
ALSwitch(config-if)#no port secure
```

C.   Apply port security with a **max-mac-count** of 1 to interface Fast Ethernet 0/8.

```
ALSwitch(config)#interface fastethernet 0/8
ALSwitch(config-if)#switchport mode access
ALSwitch(config-if)#switchport port-security
ALSwitch(config-if)#switchport port-security mac-address sticky
ALSwitch(config-if)#switchport port-security maximum 1
```

1900:

```
ALSwitch(config)#interface ethernet 0/8
ALSwitch(config-if)#port secure max-mac-count 1
```

D.   Clear the MAC address table. Note: You also could have cleared individual entries.

```
ALSwitch#clear mac-address-table
```

Step 16. Verify the results.

A.   Verify that the MAC address table has been cleared.

```
ALSwitch#show mac-address-table
```

B.   Can all PCs still successfully **ping** each other? _____

C.   If not, troubleshoot the switch and PCs.

Step 17. Exit the switch.

Exit to the switch welcome screen.

```
Switch#exit
```

After you complete the previous steps, log off (by typing **exit**) and turn all the devices off. Then remove and store the cables and adapter.

Lab 7-7   Managing Switch Operating System Files (TI 6.2.7a)

Figure 7-7.1 Topology for Lab 7-7

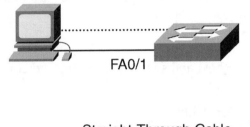

FA0/1

———— Straight-Through Cable

················· Rollover (Console) Cable

– – – – – Crossover Cable

——⌐— Serial Cable

Table 7-7.1   Lab Equipment Configuration

Switch Designation	Switch Name	VLAN 1 IP Address	Default Gateway IP Address
Switch 1	ALSwitch	192.168.1.2	192.168.1.1

The enable secret password is **class**.

The enable, VTY, and console password is **cisco**.

The subnet mask is 255.255.255.0.

Objectives

- Create and verify a basic switch configuration.

- Back up the switch IOS to a TFTP server and then restore it.

Background/Preparation

Cable a network that is similar to the one in Figure 7-7.1. The 2950 switch produced the configuration output in this lab. Another switch might produce different output. Instructions are also provided for the 1900 Series switch, which initially displays a User Interface Menu. Select the **Command Line** option from the menu to perform the steps for this lab.

Start a HyperTerminal session.

Implement the procedure documented in Appendix B, "Erasing and Reloading the Switch," before you continue with this lab.

Step 1. Configure the switch.

Configure the host name and passwords, as well as the management VLAN 1 settings for the switch, as indicated in Table 7-7.1. If you have problems while performing this configuration, refer to Lab 7-2, "Basic Switch Configuration (TI 6.2.2)."

Step 2. Configure the host that is attached to the switch.

Configure the host to use the same subnet for addresses, masks, and the default gateway as the switch. This host will act as the TFTP server in this lab. Be sure to take note of the IP address that is assigned.

Step 3. Verify connectivity.

      A.   To verify that the host and switch are configured correctly, **ping** the switch IP address from the host.

      B.   Was the **ping** successful? _____

      C.   If the answer is no, troubleshoot the host and switch configurations.

Step 4. Start and configure the Cisco TFTP server.

      A.   The TFTP server that is indicated in Figure 7-7.2 might not be the same one that is used in this classroom. Please check with the instructor for the operating instructions for the TFTP server that is used in place of the Cisco TFTP server.

Figure 7-7.2 TFTP Server Startup

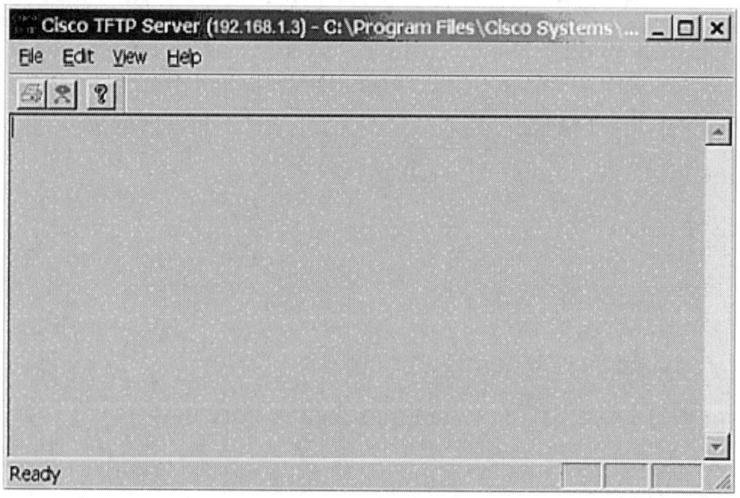

      B.   After the TFTP server is running and shows the proper address configured on the workstation, proceed to the actual copying of the Cisco IOS Software image file to the switch.

Step 5. Copy the IOS image to the TFTP server (1900: skip to Step 9).

      A.   Before you try to copy the files, verify that the TFTP server is running and **ping** the server from the switch.

      B.   What is the IP address of the TFTP server? _____

      C.   From the console session, enter **show flash**.

      D.   What is the name and length of the IOS image that is stored in Flash memory?

                        _____

      E.   What attributes can you identify from codes in the IOS filename?

                        _____

F. From the console session in the privileged EXEC mode, enter the **copy flash tftp** command. At the prompt, enter the IP address of the TFTP server.

```
ALSwitch#copy flash tftp
Source filename []? c2950-c3h2s-mz.120-5.3.WC.1.bin
Address or name of remote host []? 192.168.1.3
Destination filename [c2950-c3h2s-mz.120-5.3.WC.1.bin]?[Enter]
!!!!!!!!!!!!!!!!!!!!!!!!!!!!!!!!!!!!!!!!!!!!!!!!!!!!!!!!!!!!!!!!!!!!!!!!
!!!!!!!!!!!!!!!!!!!!!!!!!!!!!!!!!!!!!!!!!!!!!!!!!!!!!!!!!!!!!!!!!!!!!!!!
!!!!!!!!!!!!!!!!!!!!!!!!!!!!!!!!!!!!!!!!!!!!!!!!!!!!!!!!!!!!!!!!!!!!!!!!
!!!!!!!!!!!!!!!!!!!!!!!!!!!!!!!!!!!!!!!!!!!!!!!!!!!!!!!!!!!!!!!!!!!!!!!!
!!!!!!!!!!!!!!!!!!!!!!!!!!!!!!!!!!!!!!!!!!!!!!!WC!!!!!!!!!!!!!!!!!!!!!!
1674921 bytes copied in 29.952 secs (57755 bytes/sec)
ALSwitch#
```

Step 6. Verify the transfer to the TFTP server.

A. Verify the transfer by clicking **View>Log File** to check the TFTP server log file. The output should look something like the following:

```
Mon Sep 16 14:10:08 2002: Receiving 'c2950-c3h2s-mz.120-
5.3.WC.1.bin' in binary mode
Mon Sep 16 14:11:14 2002: Successful.
```

B. Verify the Flash image size in the TFTP server directory. To locate it, click on **View>Options**. This shows the TFTP server root directory. It should be similar to this, unless the default directories were changed:

C:\Program Files\Cisco Systems\Cisco TFTP Server

C. Locate this directory by using the File Manager and look at the detail listing of the file. The file length in the **show flash** command should be the same file size as the file stored on the TFTP server. If the file sizes are not identical, check with your instructor.

Step 7. Copy the IOS image from the TFTP server.

A. Now that the IOS image is backed up, the image must be tested and the IOS image must be restored to the switch. Verify again that the TFTP server is running, sharing a network with the switch, and can be reached by pinging the TFTP server IP address.

B. Record the IP address of the TFTP server. _____

C. Now start the actual copying, from the privileged EXEC prompt. Do *not* interrupt the process!

```
ALSwitch#copy tftp flash
Address or name of remote host []? 192.168.1.3
Source filename []? c2950-c3h2s-mz.120-5.3.WC.1.bin
Destination filename [c2950-c3h2s-mz.120-5.3.WC.1.bin]? [Enter]
%Warning: There is a file already existing with this name
Do you want to over write? [confirm] [Enter]
Accessing tftp://192.168.1.3/c2950-c3h2s-mz.120-5.3.WC.1.bin...
```

```
Loading c2950-c3h2s-mz.120-5.3.WC.1.bin from 192.168.1.3 (via
VLAN1):
!!!!!!!!!!!!!!!!!!!!!!!!!!!!!!!!!!!!!!!!!!!!!!!!!!!!!!!!!!!!!!!!!!!!!!!!
!!!!!!!!!!!!!!!!!!!!!!!!!!!!!!!!!!!!!!!!!!!!!!!!!!!!!!!!!!!!!!!!!!!!!!!!
!!!!!!!!!!!!!!!!!!!!!!!!!!!!!!!!!!!!!!!!!!!!!!!!!!!!!!!!!!!!!!!!!!!!!!!!
!!!!!!!!!!!!!!!!!!!!!!!!!!!!!!!!!!!!!!!!!!!!!!!!!!!!!!!!!!!!!!!!!!!!!!!!
!!!!!!!!!!!!!!!!!!!!!!!!!!!!!!!!!!!!!!!
[OK - 1674921 bytes]

1674921 bytes copied in 51.732 secs (32841 bytes/sec)
ALSwitch#
```

D.   The switch might prompt you to overwrite Flash. Will the image fit in available
       Flash?

_____

E.   What is the size of the file that is being loaded?

_____

F.   What happened on the switch console screen as the file was being downloaded?

_____

_____

G.   Was the verification successful? _____

H.   Was the whole operation successful? _____ _____

Step 8. Test the restored IOS image.

To verify that the switch IOS image is correct, cycle the switch power and observe the startup
process to confirm that there were no Flash errors. If there were no errors, then the switch's IOS
image should have started correctly. Also, to further verify the IOS image in Flash, issue the
show version command, which shows output similar to the following:

```
System image file is "flash:c2950-c3h2s-mz.120-5.3.WC.1.bin"
```

Step 9. Catalyst 1900 firmware upgrade using TFTP.

A.   Select option **F** to go to the Firmware Configuration menu from the Main Menu.
       An example of the Firmware Configuration Menu is:

```
           Catalyst 1900 - Firmware Configuration

     -------------------- System Information -------------------------
     FLASH:  1024K bytes
     V8.01.00    : Enterprise Edition
     Upgrade status:
     No upgrade currently in progress.

     -------------------- Settings -----------------------------------
     [S] TFTP Server name or IP address            192.168.1.3
     [F] Filename for firmware upgrades            cat1900.bin
     [A] Accept upgrade transfer from other hosts  Enabled
```

```
------------------- Actions -----------------------------------
    [U] System XMODEM upgrade              [D] Download test subsystem
(XMODEM)
    [T] System TFTP upgrade                [X] Exit to Main Menu
```

B.   Ensure that the switch firmware upgrade file is available on the TFTP server in the default directory. The file can be copied from another networking device or computer or it can be downloaded to the server from an appropriate website.

C.   Select option **S** from the Firmware Configuration menu and enter the IP address of the server where the switch upgrade file is located.

D.   Select option **F** from the Firmware Configuration menu and enter the name of the firmware-upgrade file.

E.   Select **T** from the Firmware Configuration menu to initiate the upgrade.

F.   Verify the upgrade is in progress by checking the Upgrade status section of the Firmware Configuration Menu. If the upgrade is in progress, the field reads "in-progress."

G.   When the transfer is complete, the switch resets automatically and executes the newly downloaded firmware.

Caution: During the transfer of the upgrade file, the switch might not respond to commands for as long as one minute. This is normal and correct. If you interrupt the transfer by turning the switch off and on, the firmware could be corrupted.

After you complete the previous steps, log off (by typing **exit**) and turn all the devices off. Then remove and store the cables and adapter.

Lab 7-8   Managing Switch Startup Configuration Files (TI 6.2.7b)

Figure 7-8.1 Topology for Lab 7-8

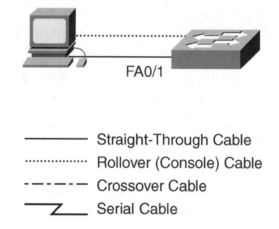

FA0/1

——————— Straight-Through Cable

················ Rollover (Console) Cable

– – – – – Crossover Cable

——Z— Serial Cable

Table 7-8.1   Lab Equipment Configuration

Switch Designation	Switch Name	VLAN 1 IP Address	Default Gateway IP Address
Switch 1	ALSwitch	192.168.1.2	192.168.1.1

The enable secret password is **class**.

The enable, VTY, and console password is **cisco**.

The subnet mask is 255.255.255.0.

Objectives

- Create and verify a basic switch configuration.

- Back up the switch startup configuration file to a TFTP server and then restore it.

Background/Preparation

Cable a network that is similar to the one in Figure 7-8.1. The 2950 switch produced the configuration output in this lab. Another switch might produce different output. Instructions are also provided for the 1900 Series switch, which initially displays a User Interface Menu. Select the **Command Line** option from the menu to perform the steps for this lab.

Start a HyperTerminal session.

Implement the procedure documented in Appendix B, "Erasing and Reloading the Switch," before you continue with this lab.

Step 1. Configure the switch.

Configure the host name and passwords, as well as the management VLAN 1 settings for the switch, as indicated in Table 7-8.1. If you have problems while performing this configuration, refer to Lab 7-2, "Basic Switch Configuration (TI 6.2.2)."

Step 2. Configure the host that is attached to the switch.

Configure the host to use the same subnet for addresses, masks, and the default gateway as the switch. This host will act as the TFTP server in this lab. Be sure to take note of the IP address that is assigned.

Step 3. Verify connectivity.

A.   To verify that the host and switch are correctly configured, **ping** the switch IP address from the host.

B.   Was the **ping** successful? _____

C.   If the answer is no, troubleshoot the host and switch configurations.

Step 4. Start and configure the Cisco TFTP server.

A.   The TFTP server that is indicated in Figure 7-8.2 might not be the same one that is used in this classroom. Please check with the instructor for the operating instructions for the TFTP server that is used in place of the Cisco TFTP server.

Figure 7-8.2 TFTP Server Startup

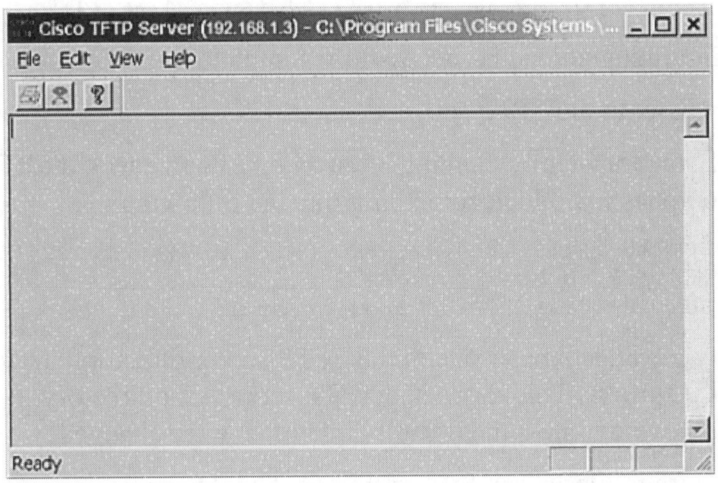

B.   After the TFTP server is running and shows the proper address configured on the workstation, proceed to the copying of the configuration file to the switch.

Step 5. Copy the startup configuration file to the TFTP server.

A.   Before you try to copy the files, verify that the TFTP server is running.

B.   What is the IP address of the TFTP server? _____

C.   From the console session, enter **show flash**.

For a 2900 switch use the command: **dir flash:**

Note: This function is not supported on the 1900 switch.

D.   What is the name and length of the startup configuration image that is stored in Flash? _____

E.   From the console session in the privileged EXEC mode, enter **copy running-config startup-config** to make sure that the running configuration file is saved to the startup configuration file. Then type the **copy startup-config tftp** command. At the prompt, enter the IP address of the TFTP server.

```
ALSwitch#copy running-config startup-config
Destination filename [startup-config]?[Enter]
Building configuration...
[OK]

ALSwitch#copy start tftp
Address or name of remote host []? 192.168.1.3
Destination filename [alswitch-confg]?[Enter]
!!
744 bytes copied in 1.60 secs (744 bytes/sec)
ALSwitch#
```

F.   Procedure for the 1900 switch.

For the 1900 switch use this procedure to copy the switch configuration file to a TFTP server.

```
ALSwitch#copy  nvram  tftp://192.168.1.3/alswitch-config
```

Configuration upload is successfully completed

Step 6. Verify the transfer to the TFTP server.

A.   Verify the transfer by clicking **View>Log File** to check the TFTP server log file. The output should look something like the following:

```
Mon Sep 16 14:10:08 2002: Receiving 'switch.confg' file from
192.168.1.2 in binary mode
Mon Sep 16 14:11:14 2002: Successful.
```

B.   Verify the Flash image size in the TFTP server directory. To locate it, click on **View>Options**. This shows the TFTP server root directory. It should be similar to the following, unless the default directories were changed.

C:\Program Files\Cisco Systems\Cisco TFTP Server

C.   Locate this directory by using the File Manager and look at the detail listing of the file. The file length in the **show flash** command should be the same file size as the file that is stored on the TFTP server. If the file sizes are not identical, check with your instructor.

Step 7. Restore the startup configuration file from the TFTP server.

A.   Erase the switch startup configuration file. Then reconfigure it with just the VLAN 1 IP address of 192.168.1.2 255.255.255.0. After that, type the command

copy tftp startup-config at the privileged EXEC mode prompt. Do *not* interrupt the process!

```
Switch#copy tftp startup-config
Address or name of remote host []? 192.168.1.3
Destination filename [switch-confg]?[Enter]
```

```
!!
744 bytes copied in 0.40 secs
Switch#copy tftp startup-config
Address or name of remote host []? 192.168.1.3
Source filename []? switch-confg
Destination filename [startup-config]?
Accessing tftp://192.168.1.3/switch-confg...
Loading switch-confg from 192.168.1.3 (via VLAN1): !
[OK - 744 bytes]
[OK]
744 bytes copied in 0.100 secs
Switch#
```

Was the operation successful? _____

F.   Procedure for the 1900 switch

For the 1900 switch use this procedure to copy the switch configuration file to a TFTP server.

```
ALSwitch#copy  tftp://192.168.1.3/alswitch-config nvram

TFTP successfully downloaded configuration file
```

Step 8. Test the restored startup configuration image (not supported on the 1900).

To verify that the switch image is correct, cycle the switch power and observe the switch prompt. If it has returned to the name that was assigned to it in the original configuration, the restoration is complete. Type the command **show startup-config** to see the restored configuration.

After you complete the previous steps, log off (by typing **exit**) and turn all the devices off. Then remove and store the cables and adapter.

Lab 7-9 Password Recovery Procedure for a Catalyst 2900 Series Switch (TI 6.2.8)

Figure 7-9.1 Topology for Lab 7-9

FA0/1

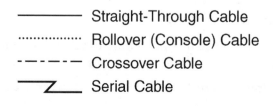

——————— Straight-Through Cable

················· Rollover (Console) Cable

– – – – – Crossover Cable

———Z—— Serial Cable

Table 7-9.1   Lab Equipment Configuration

Switch Designation	Switch Name	VLAN 1 IP Address	Default Gateway IP Address
Switch 1	ALSwitch	192.168.1.2	192.168.1.1

The enable secret password is **class**.
The enable, VTY, and console password is **cisco**.
The subnet mask is 255.255.255.0.

Objectives

- Create a basic switch configuration and verify it.

- Change passwords so that the password recovery procedure must be performed.

Background/Preparation

Cable a network that is similar to the one in Figure 7-9.1. The 2950 switch produced the configuration output in this lab. Another switch might produce different output. Instructions are also provided for the 1900 Series switch, which initially displays a User Interface Menu. Select the **Command Line** option from the menu to perform the steps for this lab.

Start a HyperTerminal session.

Implement the procedure documented in Appendix B, "Erasing and Reloading the Switch," before you continue with this lab.

Step 1. Configure the switch.

Configure the host name and passwords, as well as the management VLAN 1 settings for the switch, as indicated in Table 7-9.1. If you have problems while performing this configuration, refer to Lab 7-2, "Basic Switch Configuration (TI 6.2.2)."

Step 2. Configure the host that is attached to the switch.

Configure the host to use the same subnet for addresses, masks, and the default gateway as the switch.

Step 3. Verify connectivity.

    A.   To verify that the host and switch are correctly configured, **ping** the switch IP address from the host.

    B.   Was the **ping** successful? _____

    C.   If the answer is no, troubleshoot the host and switch configurations.

Step 4. Reset the Console Password.

    A.   Have a classmate change the console and vty passwords on the switch, save the changes to the **startup-config** file, and reload the switch.

    B.   Without knowing the passwords, try to gain access to the switch.

Step 5. Recover Access to the Switch.

    A.   Make sure that a PC is connected to the console port and a HyperTerminal window is open.

    B.   Power off the switch and turn it back on while holding down the MODE button on the front of the switch at the same time that the switch is powered on. Release the MODE button a few seconds after the STAT LED is no longer lit.

    C.   The following should be displayed, which includes information on which commands to use next:

```
C2950 Boot Loader (C2950-HBOOT-M) Version 12.1(11r)EA1, RELEASE
SOFTWARE (fc1)
Compiled Mon 22-Jul-02 18:57 by antonino
WS-C2950-24 starting...
Base ethernet MAC Address: 00:0a:b7:72:2b:40
Xmodem file system is available.
The system has been interrupted prior to initializing the Flash
file system. The following commands initialize the flash file
system and finish loading the operating system software:
    flash_init
    load_helper
    boot
```

    D.   To initialize the file system and finish loading the operating system,

               Type **flash_init**.

               Type **load_helper**.

               Type **dir flash:** (Do not forget to type the : (colon) after the word *flash.*)

    E.   Type **rename flash:config.text flash:config.old** to rename the configuration file.

               This file contains the password definition.

Step 6. Restart the System.

    A.   Type **boot** to boot the system.

    B.   Enter **N** at the prompt to start the Setup program.

```
Continue with the configuration dialog? [yes/no] : N
```

    C.   Type **rename flash:config.old flash:config.text** to rename the configuration file with its original name at the privileged EXEC mode prompt.

    D.   Copy the configuration file into memory:

```
Switch#copy flash:config.text system:running-config
Source filename [config.text]?[Enter]
Destination filename [running-config][Enter]
```

    E.   The configuration file is now reloaded, so change the old unknown passwords and save the new configuration.

```
ALSwitch#configure terminal
ALSwitch(config)#no enable secret
ALSwitch(config)#enable password cisco
Switch(config)#enable secret class
ALSwitch(config)#line console 0
ALSwitch(config-line)#password cisco
ALSwitch(config-line)#exit
ALSwitch(config)#line vty 0 15
ALSwitch(config-line)#password cisco
ALSwitch(config-line)#exit
ALSwitch(config)#exit
ALSwitch#copy running-config startup-config
Destination filename [startup-config]?[Enter]
Building configuration...
[OK]
ALSwitch#
```

    F.   Power cycle the switch and verify that the passwords are now functional.

                If not, repeat the procedure.

                After you complete the previous steps, log off (by typing **exit**) and turn all the devices off. Then remove and store the cables and adapter.

Step 7. Procedure for the 1900 and 2800 switches.

    A.   Check the boot firmware version number from the Systems Engineering menu. To access the Systems Engineering menu, follow the procedure below:

            1.   Disconnect the power cord from the rear panel.

            2.   Press and hold the **Mode** button on the front panel.

            3.   Power-cycle the switch.

4.   Release the **Mode** button one or two seconds after LED above port 1x goes off or when the diagnostic console is displayed.

```
Cisco Systems Diagnostic Console
Copyright(c) Cisco Systems, Inc. 1999
All rights reserved.

Ethernet Address: 00-E0-1E-7E-B4-40
--------------------------------------------------
```

Press **Enter** to continue.

5.   Press **Enter** to display the **Diagnostic Console - Systems Engineering** menu.

You will see the following **Systems Engineering** menu:

```
Diagnostic Console - Systems Engineering
Operation firmware version: 8.00.00 Status: valid
Boot firmware version: 3.02
[C] Continue with standard system start up
[U] Upgrade operation firmware (XMODEM)
[S] System Debug Interface
Enter Selection:
```

6.   The **bold** letters above show the Boot firmware version.

B.   Clearing the password (firmware version 1.10 and later)

To clear your password, follow the steps below:

1.   Power-cycle the switch.

After POST completes, the following prompt displays:

```
Do you wish to clear the passwords? [Y]es or [N]o:
```

Note: You have 10 seconds to respond. If you don't respond within that time, the **Management Console Logon** screen appears. You cannot change this waiting period.

2.   Enter **Y** to delete the existing password from Nonvolatile RAM (NVRAM).

Note: If you type **N**, the existing password remains valid.

3.   Assign a password from the switch management interfaces (management console or Command Line Interface (CLI)).

C.   Viewing the password (firmware versions between 1.10 and 3.02)

For firmware versions between 1.10 and 3.02, you can view the password you are trying to recover (instead of clearing it as described in the previous section).

1.   Access the diagnostic console.

a.   Press and hold the **Mode** button.

b.   Power-cycle the switch.

c.   Release the **Mode** button one or two seconds after LED above port 1x goes off or the diagnostics console appears.

You will see the following logon screen:

```
--------------------------------------------------
Cisco Systems Diagnostic Console
Copyright(c) Cisco Systems, Inc. 1999
All rights reserved.


Ethernet Address: 00-E0-1E-7E-B4-40
--------------------------------------------------
```

d.   Press **Enter** to continue.

2.   Press **Enter** and select the **[S]** option on the **Diagnostic Console - Systems Engineering menu**, and then select the **[V]** option on the **Diagnostic Console - System Debug Interface** menu to display the management console password.

3.   If you want to change the password, select the **[M]** option on the **Console Settings** menu.

D.   Password recovery for firmware version 1.09 and earlier.

Note: If the shipping date is before June 1997, gather the information listed in this section, and contact the Cisco Technical Assistance Center (TAC) for password recovery.

Note: This section is also applicable for those Catalyst 2800 switches that do not have the **Mode** button in their front panel.

To recover your password, follow the steps below:

1.   Contact the Cisco TAC for the factory-installed password.

2.   Provide the serial number or Media Access Control (MAC) address of the switch.

The serial number is usually located on the back of the unit. To obtain the MAC address, remove the cover and read the Ethernet address of the Programmable Read-Only Memory (PROM).

Lab 7-10 Firmware Upgrade of a Catalyst 2900 Series Switch (TI 6.2.9)

Figure 7-10.1 Topology for Lab 7-10

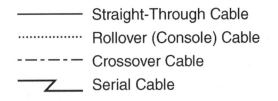

FA0/1

————— Straight-Through Cable

··············· Rollover (Console) Cable

– – – – – Crossover Cable

⎺⎺Z⎽⎽ Serial Cable

Table 7-10.1 Lab Equipment Configuration

Switch Designation	Switch Name	VLAN 1 IP Address	Default Gateway IP Address
Switch 1	ALSwitch	192.168.1.2	192.168.1.1

The enable secret password is **class**.

The enable, VTY, and console password is **cisco**.

The subnet mask is 255.255.255.0.

Objectives

- Create a basic switch configuration and verify it.

- Upgrade the IOS and HTML files from a file that the instructor supplies.

Background/Preparation

Cable a network that is similar to the one in Figure 7-10.1. The 2950 switch produced the configuration output in this lab. Another switch might produce different output.

Start a HyperTerminal session.

Implement the procedure documented in Appendix B, "Erasing and Reloading the Switch," before you continue with this lab.

Important notes:

This lab requires that a combined IOS image and HTML file **c2950-i6q4l2-tar.121-22.EA1.tar** be in the default file directory of the TFTP server. The instructor should download this file or a more current one from the Cisco Connection online software center. The IOS update release contains new HTML files to support changes to the web interface.

This lab requires that there be a saved copy of the current configuration file as backup.

Step 1. Configure the switch.

Configure the host name and passwords, as well as the management VLAN 1 settings for the switch, as indicated in Table 7-10.1. If you have problems while performing this configuration, refer to Lab 7-2, "Basic Switch Configuration (TI 6.2.2)."

Step 2. Configure the host that is attached to the switch.

Configure the host to use the same IP subnet for addresses, masks, and the default gateway as the switch.

Step 3. Verify connectivity.

A.   To verify that the host and switch are correctly configured, **ping** the switch IP address from the host.

B.   Was the **ping** successful? _____

C.   If the answer is no, troubleshoot the host and switch configurations.

Step 4. Display the name of the running image file.

A.   Display the name of the running image file by using the **show boot** command from the privileged EXEC mode prompt.

```
ALSwitch#show boot
BOOT path-list:
Config file:            flash:config.text
Enable Break:           no
Manual Boot:            no
HELPER path-list:
NVRAM/Config file
buffer size:                 32768
ALSwitch#
```

B.   If, as above, no software image is defined in the boot path, enter **dir flash:** or **show flash** to display the contents:

```
ALSwitch#dir flash:
Directory of flash:/

2 -rwx 1674921 Mar 01 1993 01:28:10 c2950-c3h2s-mz.120-
5.3.WC.1.bin
3 -rwx 269 Jan 01 1970 00:00:57 env_vars
4 drwx 10240 Mar 01 1993 00:21:13 html
165-rwx 965 Mar 01 1993 00:22:23 config.text

7741440 bytes total (4778496 bytes free)
```

Step 5. Prepare for the new image.

A. If the switch has enough free memory as shown in the previous step, rename the existing IOS image file to the same name with the .old extension. If there is not enough memory, make sure that a copy of the IOS image exists on the TFTP server.

```
ALSwitch#rename flash:c2950-c3h2s-mz.120-5.3.WC.1.bin
flash:c2950-c3h2s-mz.120-5.3.WC.1.old
```

B. Verify that the renaming was successful.

```
ALSwitch#dir flash:
Directory of flash:/

 2 -rwx 1674921 Mar 01 1993 01:28:10 c2950-c3h2s-mz.120-
5.3.WC.1.old
 3 -rwx 269 Jan 01 1970 00:00:57 env_vars
 4 drwx 10240 Mar 01 1993 00:21:13 html
167 -rwx 965 Mar 01 1993 00:22:23 config.text

7741440 bytes total (4778496 bytes free)
ALSwitch#
```

C. As a precaution, disable access to the switch HTML pages.

```
ALSwitch(config)#no ip http server
```

D. Remove existing html files from the flash: directory

```
ALSwitch#delete flash:html/*
```

Step 6. Extract the new IOS image and HTML files into Flash memory.

A. Use the **tar** command as shown:

```
ALSwitch#archive tar /x tftp://192.168.1.3//c2950-i6q4l2-tar.121-
22.EA1.tar flash:
```

Note: Depending on the TFTP server that is being used, you might need only one slash (/) after the IP address of the server. The name of the file to extract may also be different depending on which one the instructor downloaded.

B. Re-enable access to the switch HTML pages.

```
ALSwitch(config)#ip http server
```

Step 7. Associate the new boot file.

Enter the **boot** command with the name of the *new image* filename at the configuration mode prompt.

```
ALSwitch(config)#boot system flash:c2950-i6q4l2-tar.121-22.EA1.tar
```

Step 8. Restart the switch.

A. Restart the switch by using the **reload** command to see if the new IOS loaded. Use the **show version** command to see the IOS filename.

B.   What was the name of the IOS file that the switch booted from? _____

C.   Was this the proper filename? _____

Step 9. Restart the switch.

A.   Restart the switch by using the **reload** command to see if the new IOS loaded. Use the **show version** command to see the IOS filename.

B.   What was the name of the IOS file that the switch booted from? _____

C.   Was this the proper filename? _____

D.   If the IOS filename is correct, remove the backup file from Flash memory by using the command **delete flash:c2950-c3h2s-mz.120-5.3.WC.1.old** (or whatever the name of the you renamed was) from the privileged EXEC mode prompt.

After you complete the previous steps, log off (by typing **exit**) and turn all the devices off. Then remove and store the cables and adapter.

CCNA 3

Chapter 8: Spanning Tree Protocol (STP)

The following table maps the numbering scheme that is used in this chapter's labs to the Target Indicators (TIs) that are used in the online curriculum.

Lab Companion Numbering	Online Curriculum TI
Lab 8-1	7.2.4
Lab 8-2	7.2.6

Lab 8-1   Selecting the Root Bridge (TI 7.2.4)

Figure 8-1.1 Topology for Lab 8-1

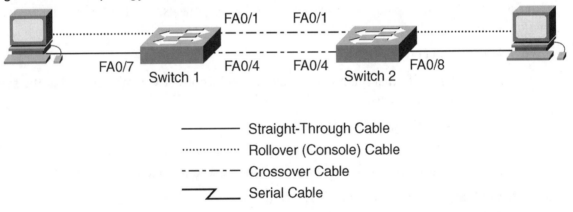

————— Straight-Through Cable

················ Rollover (Console) Cable

– – – – – Crossover Cable

⌇⌇ Serial Cable

Table 8-1.1   Lab Equipment Configuration

Switch Designation	Switch Name	VLAN 1 IP Address	Default Gateway IP Address
Switch 1	Switch_A	192.168.1.2	192.168.1.1
Switch 2	Switch_B	192.168.1.3	192.168.1.1

The enable secret password for both switches is **class**.
The enable, VTY, and console password for both switches is **cisco**.
The subnet mask for both switches is 255.255.255.0.

Objectives

- Create a basic switch configuration and verify it.

- Determine which switch is selected as a root switch with factory default settings.

- Force the other switch to be selected as a root switch.

Background/Preparation

Cable a network that is similar to the one in Figure 8-1.1. The 2950 series switch produced the configuration output in this lab. Another switch might produce different output. You should execute the following steps on each switch unless you are specifically instructed otherwise.

Start a HyperTerminal session.

Implement the procedure that is documented in Appendix B, "Erasing and Reloading the Switch," on all switches before you continue with this lab.

Step 1. Configure the switches.

Configure the host names and passwords, as well as the management VLAN 1 settings for each switch, as indicated in Table 8-1.1. If you have problems while performing this configuration, refer to Lab 7-2, "Basic Switch Configuration (TI 6.2.2.)."

Step 2. Configure the hosts that are attached to the switches.

Configure the host to use the same subnet for addresses, masks, and the default gateway as the switch.

Step 3. Verify connectivity.

A.   To verify that the hosts and switches are correctly configured, **ping** the switches from the hosts.

B.   Were the **ping**s successful?

_____

C.   If the answer is no, troubleshoot the hosts and switches configurations.

Step 4. Look at the show interface VLAN options.

A.   Type **show interface vlan 1 ?** .

B.   List some of the options that are available. _____ _____

_____

Step 5. Look at the VLAN interface information.

A.   On Switch_A, type the command **show interface VLAN1** at the privileged EXEC mode prompt.

```
Switch_A#show interface vlan 1
```

B.   What is the MAC address of the switch? _____

C.   On Switch_B, type the command **show interface VLAN1** at the privileged EXEC mode prompt.

```
Switch_B#show interface vlan 1
```

D.   What is the MAC address of the switch? _____

E.   Which switch should be the root of the spanning tree for VLAN 1?

_____

Step 6. Look at the switches spanning tree table.

A.   On Switch_A, type **show spanning-tree brief** at the privileged EXEC mode prompt if you are running Cisco IOS Software Release 12.0. If you are running Cisco IOS Software Release 12.1, type **show spanning-tree**.

```
Switch_A#show spanning-tree brief
```

B.   On Switch_B, type **show spanning-tree brief** at the privileged EXEC mode prompt.

```
Switch_B#show spanning-tree brief
```

C.   Examine your output and answer the following questions.

Which switch is the root switch? _____

What is the priority of the root switch? _____

What is the bridge ID of the root switch? _____

Which ports are forwarding on the root switch? _____

Which ports are blocking on the root switch? _____

What is the priority of the non-root switch? _____

What is the bridge id of the non-root switch? _____

Which ports are forwarding on the non-root switch? _____

Which ports are blocking on the non-root switch? _____

What is the status of the link light on the blocking port? _____

Step 7. Reassign the root bridge.

A.   The switch that has been selected as the root bridge, by using default values, is not the best choice. You must force the "other" switch to become the root switch.

In the previous example output, the root switch by default is Switch_A. Switch_B is preferred as the root switch. Go to the console and enter configuration mode if necessary.

B.   Determine the parameters that you can configure for the spanning-tree protocol.

```
Switch_B(config)#spanning-tree ?
```

C.   List the options. _____ _____ _____

_____ _____ _____

_____

D.   Set the priority of the switch that is not root to 4096.

If you are using Cisco IOS Software Release 12.0:

```
Switch_B(config)#spanning-tree priority 1
Switch_B(config)#exit
```

If you are using Cisco IOS Software Release 12.1:

```
Switch_B(config)#spanning-tree vlan 1 priority 4096
Switch_B(config)#exit
```

Step 8. Look at the switch spanning tree table.

A. On Switch_A, type **show spanning-tree brief** at the privileged EXEC mode prompt if you are running Cisco IOS Software Release 12.0. If you are running Cisco IOS Software Release 12.1, type **show spanning-tree**.

```
Switch_A#show spanning-tree brief
```

B. On Switch_B, type **show spanning-tree brief** at the privileged EXEC mode prompt.

```
Switch_B#show spanning-tree brief
```

C. Examine your output and answer the following questions.

Which switch is the root switch? _____

What is the priority of the root switch? _____

Which ports are forwarding on the root switch? _____

Which ports are blocking on the root switch? _____

What is the priority of the non-root switch? _____

Which ports are forwarding on the non-root switch? _____

Which ports are blocking on the non-root switch? _____

What is the status of the link light on the blocking port? _____

Step 9. Verify the running configuration file on the root switch.

A. On the switch that was changed to be the root bridge, type **show running-config** at the privileged EXEC mode prompt.

B. Does an entry exist in the running configuration file that specifies this router's spanning tree priority?

_____

C. What does that entry say? _____

Note: The output is different depending on whether the Cisco IOS is Release 12.0 or Release 12.1.

After you complete the previous steps, log off (by typing **exit**) and turn all the devices off. Then remove and store the cables and adapter.

Lab 8-2   Spanning Tree Recalculation (TI 7.2.6)

Figure 8-2.1   Topology for Lab 8-2

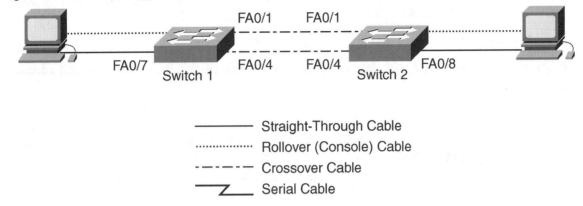

——————— Straight-Through Cable

················· Rollover (Console) Cable

— — — — — Crossover Cable

—————ᐱ——— Serial Cable

Table 8-2.1   Lab Equipment Configuration

Switch Designation	Switch Name	VLAN 1 IP Address	Default Gateway IP Address
Switch 1	Switch_A	192.168.1.2	192.168.1.1
Switch 2	Switch_B	192.168.1.3	192.168.1.1

The enable secret password for both switches is **class**.

The enable, VTY, and console password for both switches is **cisco**.

The subnet mask for both switches is 255.255.255.0.

Objectives

- Create a basic switch configuration and verify it.

- Observe the behavior of the Spanning Tree Algorithm in the presence of switched network topology changes.

Background/Preparation

Cable a network that is similar to the one in Figure 8-2.1. The 2950 series switch produced the configuration output in this lab. Another switch might produce different output. You should execute the following steps on each switch unless you are specifically instructed otherwise.

Start a HyperTerminal session.

Implement the procedure documented in Appendix B on all switches before you continue with this lab.

Step 1. Configure the switches.

Configure the host names and passwords, as well as the management VLAN 1 settings for each switch, as indicated in Table 8-2.1. If you have problems while performing this configuration, refer to Lab 7-2, "Basic Switch Configuration (TI 6.2.2)."

Step 2. Configure the hosts that are attached to the switches.

Configure the host to use the same IP subnet for addresses, masks, and the default gateway as the switch.

Step 3. Verify connectivity.

    A.   To verify that the hosts and switches are configured correctly, **ping** the switches from the hosts.

    B.   Were the **ping**s successful? _____

    C.   If the answer is no, troubleshoot the hosts and switches configurations.

Step 4. Look at the VLAN interface information.

    A.   On both switches, type the command **show interface vlan 1** at the privileged EXEC prompt.

```
Switch_A#show interface vlan 1
```

    B.   What is the MAC address of the switch? _____

```
Switch_B#show interface vlan 1
```

    C.   What is the MAC address of the switch? _____

    D.   Which switch should be the root of the spanning tree for VLAN 1?

_____

Step 5. Look at the switches spanning tree table.

    A.   On Switch_A, type **show spanning-tree brief** at the privileged EXEC mode prompt if you are running Cisco IOS Software Release 12.0. If you are running Cisco IOS Software Release 12.1, type **show spanning-tree**. Different releases of IOS have different options for this command.

```
Switch_A#show spanning-tree brief
```

    B.   On Switch_B, type **show spanning-tree brief** at the privileged EXEC mode prompt.

```
Switch_B#show spanning-tree brief
```

    C.   Examine the command output and answer the following questions.

Which switch is the root switch? _____

Record the states of the first 12 interfaces and ports of each switch in Table 8-2.2.

Table 8-2.2   Switch Interface/Port States

Switch_A	Port #	Switch_B
	1	
	2	
	3	
	4	
	5	
	6	
	7	
	8	
	9	
	10	
	11	
	12	

Step 6. Remove a cable on the switch.

A.   Remove the cable from the forwarding port on the non-root switch. For the previous example, this is interface Fast Ethernet 0/1 on Switch_B.

B.   Wait for at least two minutes.

C.   What has happened to the switch port LEDs?

_____

Step 7. Look at the spanning tree table for the switches.

A.   On Switch_A, type **show spanning-tree brief** at the privileged EXEC mode prompt if you are running Cisco IOS Software Release 12.0. If you are running Cisco IOS Software Release 12.1, type **show spanning-tree**. Different releases of IOS have different options for this command.

```
Switch_A#show spanning-tree brief
```

B.   On Switch_B, type **show spanning-tree brief** at the privileged EXEC mode prompt.

```
Switch_B#show spanning-tree brief
```

C.   What changes have taken place in the command output?

On Switch_A?

_____

On Switch_B?

_____

Step 8. Replace the cable in the switch

A.   Replace the cable in the port that it was removed from. For the previous example, this is interface Fast Ethernet 0/1 on Switch_B.

B.   Wait for at least two minutes.

C.   What has happened to the switch port LEDs?

_____

Step 9. Look at the spanning tree table for the switches.

A.   On Switch_A, type **show spanning-tree brief** at the privileged EXEC mode prompt if you are running Cisco IOS Software Release 12.0. If you are running Cisco IOS Software Release 12.1, type **show spanning-tree**. Different releases of IOS have different options for this command.

```
Switch_A#show spanning-tree brief
```

B.   On Switch_B, type **show spanning-tree brief** at the privileged EXEC mode prompt.

```
Switch_B#show spanning-tree brief
```

C.   What changes have taken place in the command output?

On Switch_A?

_____

On Switch_B?

_____

After you complete the previous steps, log off (by typing **exit**) and turn all the devices off. Then remove and store the cables and adapter.

Part II   CCNA 4 Labs: WAN Technologies

CCNA4

Chapter 11: Scaling IP Addresses

The following table maps the numbering scheme that is used in this chapter's labs to the Target Indicators (TIs) that are used in the online curriculum.

Lab Companion Numbering	Online Curriculum TI
Lab 11-1	1.1.4.a
Lab 11-2	1.1.4.b
Lab 11-3	1.1.4.c
Lab 11-4	1.1.5
Lab 11-5	1.1.6
Lab 11-6	1.2.6
Lab 11-7	1.2.8

Lab 11-1 Configuring NAT (TI 1.1.4a)

Figure 11-1.1   Topology for Lab 11-1

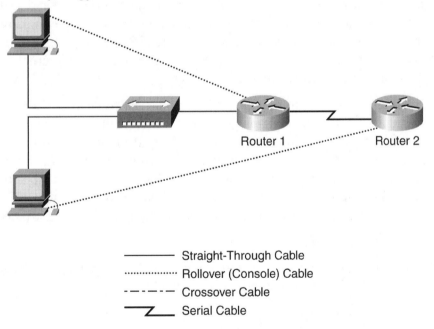

Router 1   Router 2

——————— Straight-Through Cable

·················· Rollover (Console) Cable

– – – – – Crossover Cable

⎯⎯Z⎯ Serial Cable

Table 11-1.1 Lab Equipment Configuration

Router Designation	Router Name	Fast Ethernet 0 Address/ Subnet Mask	Interface Type	Serial 0 Address/ Subnet Mask	Loopback 0 Address/ Subnet Mask
Router 1	Gateway	10.10.10.1/24	DTE	200.2.2.18/30	NA
Router 2	ISP	NA	DCE	200.2.2.17/30	172.16.1.1/32

The enable secret password for both routers is **class**.

The enable, VTY, and console password for both routers is **cisco**.

Objective

Configure a router to use Network Address Translation (NAT) to convert internal IP addresses, which are typically private addresses, into outside public addresses.

Background/Preparation

The ISP has allocated the public CIDR IP address 199.99.9.32/27 to a company. This is equivalent to 30 public IP addresses. Because the company has an internal requirement for more than 30 addresses, the IT manager has decided to implement NAT. They have decided to reserve the addresses 199.99.9.33 – 199.99.9.39 for static allocation and 199.99.9.40 – 199.99.9.62 for dynamic allocation. Routing between the ISP and the company's gateway router will be done by using a static route between the ISP and the gateway and a default route between the gateway and the ISP. The ISP's connection to the Internet will be represented by a loopback address on the ISP router.

Cable a network that is similar to the one in Figure 11-1.1. You can use any router that meets the interface requirements that are displayed in the diagram (that is, 800, 1600, 1700, 2500, and 2600 routers or a combination). Please refer to the information in Appendix C, "Router Interface Summary Chart," to correctly specify the interface identifiers to be used based on the equipment in your lab. The configuration output that is used in this lab is produced from 1721 series routers. Another router might produce slightly different output. You should execute the following steps on each router unless you are specifically instructed otherwise.

Start a HyperTerminal session.

Please refer to and implement the procedure documented in Appendix B, "Erasing and Reloading the Switch," before you continue with this lab.

Step 1. Configure the routers.

Configure the host name, console, virtual terminal and enable passwords, and the interfaces according to the chart. If you have trouble doing this, refer to the configuration reference sheet at the end of this lab.

Step 2. Save the configuration.

At the privileged EXEC mode prompt, on both routers, type the command **copy running-config startup-config.**

Step 3. Configure the hosts with the proper IP address, subnet mask, and default gateway.

Each workstation should be able to **ping** the attached router. Troubleshoot as necessary. Hint: Remember to assign a specific IP address and default gateway to the workstation. If you are running Windows 98, check using **Start>Run>winipcfg**. If you are running Windows 2000 or later, check using **ipconfig** in a DOS window.

Step 4. Verify that the network is functioning.

A.   From the attached hosts, **ping** the Fast Ethernet interface of the default gateway router.

B.   Was the **ping** from the first host successful? _____

C.   Was the **ping** from the second host successful? _____

D.   If the answer is no for either question, troubleshoot the router and host configurations to find the error. Then **ping** again until they are successful.

Step 5. Create a static route.

A.   Create a static route from the ISP to the gateway router. Addresses 199.99.9.32/27 have been allocated for Internet access outside the company. Use the **ip route** command to create the static route.

```
ISP(config)#ip route 199.99.9.32 255.255.255.224 200.2.2.18
```

B.   Is the static route in the routing table? _____

C.   What command checks the routing table contents?

_____

D.   If the route was not in the routing table, give one reason why this might be so.

_____

Step 6. Create a default route.

A.   Add a default route, using the **ip route** command, from the gateway router to the ISP router. This forwards any unknown destination address traffic to the ISP.

```
Gateway(config)#ip route 0.0.0.0 0.0.0.0 200.2.2.17
```

B.   Is the static route in the routing table? _____

C.   Try to **ping** from one of the workstations to the ISP serial interface IP address.

D.   Was the **ping** successful? _____

E.   Why?

_____

Step 7. Define the pool of usable public IP addresses.

To define the pool of public addresses, use the **ip nat pool** command.

```
Gateway(config)#ip nat pool public_access 199.99.9.40 199.99.9.62
netmask 255.255.255.224
```

Step 8. Define an access list that matches the inside private IP addresses.

To define the access list to match the inside private addresses, use the access list command.

```
Gateway(config)#access-list 1 permit 10.10.10.0 0.0.0.255
```

Step 9. Define the NAT translation from inside the list to outside the pool.

To define the NAT Translation, use the ip nat inside source command.

```
Gateway(config)#ip nat inside source list 1 pool public_access
```

Step 10. Specify the interfaces.

You must specify whether the active interfaces on the router are inside or outside interfaces with respect to NAT. To do this, use the ip nat inside or ip nat outside command.

```
Gateway(config)#interface fastethernet 0

Gateway(config-if)#ip nat inside

Gateway(config-if)#interface serial 0

Gateway(config-if)#ip nat outside
```

Step 11. Test the configuration.

A.   Configure a workstation on the internal LAN with the IP address 10.10.10.10/24 and a default gateway 10.10.10.1. From the PC, **ping** 172.16.1.1. If successful, look at the NAT translation on the gateway router by using the command **show ip nat translations**.

B.   What is the translation of the inside local host addresses?

_____ = _____ _____ = _____

C.   How is the inside global address assigned?

_____

D.   How is the inside local address assigned?

_____

After you complete the previous steps, log off (by typing **exit**) and turn the router off. Then remove and store the cables and adapter.

Configuration Reference Sheet for This Lab

This sheet contains the basic configuration commands for the ISP and gateway routers.

ISP

```
Router#configure terminal
Router(config)#hostname ISP
ISP(config)#enable password cisco
ISP(config)#enable secret class
ISP(config)#line console 0
ISP(config-line)#password cisco
ISP(config-line)#login
ISP(config-line)#exit
ISP(config)#line vty 0 4
ISP(config-line)#password cisco
ISP(config-line)#login
```

```
ISP(config-line)#exit
ISP(config)#interface loopback 0
ISP(config-if)#ip add 172.16.1.1 255.255.255.255
ISP(config-if)#no shutdown
ISP(config-if)#exit
ISP(config)#interface serial 0
ISP(config-if)#ip add 200.2.2.17 255.255.255.252
ISP(config-if)#no shutdown
ISP(config-if)#clockrate 64000
ISP(config)#ip route 199.99.9.32 255.255.255.224 200.2.2.18
ISP(config)#end
ISP#copy running-config startup-config
```

Gateway

```
Router#configure terminal
Router(config)#hostname Gateway
Gateway(config)#enable password cisco
Gateway(config)#enable secret class
Gateway(config)#line console 0
Gateway(config-line)#password cisco
Gateway(config-line)#login
Gateway(config-line)#exit
Gateway(config)#line vty 0 4
Gateway(config-line)#password cisco
Gateway(config-line)#login
Gateway(config-line)#exit
Gateway(config)#interface fastethernet 0
Gateway(config-if)#ip add 10.10.10.1  255.255.255.0
Gateway(config-if)#no shutdown
Gateway(config-if)#exit
Gateway(config)#interface serial 0
Gateway(config-if)#ip add 200.2.2.18 255.255.255.252
Gateway(config-if)#no shutdown
Gateway(config)#ip route 0.0.0.0 0.0.0.0 200.2.2.17
Gateway(config)#end
Gateway#copy running-config startup-config
```

Lab 11-2   Configuring PAT (TI 1.1.4b)

Figure 11-2.1   Topology for Lab 11-2

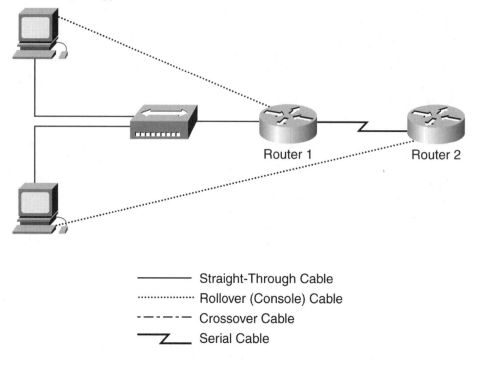

---------- Straight-Through Cable

················ Rollover (Console) Cable

– – – – – Crossover Cable

––––⌐Z–– Serial Cable

Table 11-2.1 Lab Equipment Configuration

Router Designation	Router Name	Fast Ethernet 0 Address/ Subnet Mask	Interface Type	Serial 0 Address / Subnet Mask	Loopback 0 Address/ Subnet Mask
Router 1	Gateway	10.10.10.1/24	DTE	200.2.2.18/30	NA
Router 2	ISP	NA	DCE	200.2.2.17/30	172.16.1.1/32

The enable secret password for both routers is **class**.

The enable, VTY, and console password for both routers is **cisco**.

Objective

Configure a router to use Port Address Translation (PAT) to convert internal IP addresses, which are typically private addresses, into an outside public address.

Background/Preparation

Aidan McDonald has just received a DSL line Internet connection in his home to a local ISP. The ISP has allocated only one IP address to be used on the serial port of his remote access device. Thus, all PCs on Aidan's LAN, each with its own private IP address, will share one public IP address on the router using PAT. Routing from the home or gateway router to the

ISP will be done by using a default route to Serial 0 of the Gateway router. The ISP connection to the Internet will be represented by a loopback address on the ISP router.

Cable a network that is similar to the one in Figure 11-2.1. You can use any router that meets the interface requirements that are displayed in the diagram (that is, 800, 1600, 1700, 2500, and 2600 routers or a combination). Please refer to the information in Appendix C to correctly specify the interface identifiers to be used based on the equipment in your lab. The configuration output used in this lab is produced from 1721 series routers. Another router might produce slightly different output. You should execute the following steps on each router unless you are specifically instructed otherwise.

Start a HyperTerminal session.

Please refer to and implement the procedure documented in Appendix A, "Erasing and Reloading the Router," before you continue with this lab.

Step 1. Configure the routers.

Configure the host name, console, virtual terminal and enable passwords, and the interfaces according to the chart. If you have trouble doing this, refer to Lab 11-1, "Configuring NAT (TI 1.1.4a)."

Step 2. Save the configurations.

At the privileged EXEC mode prompt on both routers, type the command **copy running-config startup-config.**

Step 3. Configure the hosts with the proper IP address, subnet mask, and default gateway.

Each workstation should be able to **ping** the attached router. Troubleshoot as necessary. Hint: Remember to assign a specific IP address and default gateway to the workstation. If you are running Windows 98, check using **Start>Run>winipcfg**. If you are running Windows 2000 or later, check using **ipconfig** in a DOS window.

Step 4. Verify that the network is functioning.

    A.   From the attached hosts, **ping** the Fast Ethernet interface of the default gateway router.

    B.   Was the **ping** from the first host successful? _____

    C.   Was the **ping** from the second host successful? _____

    D.   If the answer is no for either question, troubleshoot the router and host configurations to find the error. Then **ping** again until they are successful.

Step 5. Create a default route.

    A.   Add a default route from the gateway to the ISP router. This forwards any unknown destination address traffic to the ISP. Use the **ip route** command to create the default route.

```
Gateway(config)#ip route 0.0.0.0 0.0.0.0 200.2.2.17
```

    B.   Is the route in the routing table? _____

C.   Try to **ping** from one of the workstations to the ISP serial interface IP address.

D.   Was the **ping** successful? _____

E.   Why?

_____

F.   What command checks the routing table contents?

_____

Step 6. Define an access list that matches the inside private IP addresses.

To define the access list to match the inside private addresses, use the **access list** command.

```
Gateway(config)#access-list 1 permit 10.10.10.0 0.0.0.255
```

Step 7. Define the PAT translation from inside the list to outside the address.

To define the PAT translation, use the ip nat inside source command. This command with the overload option creates PAT by using the serial 0 IP address as the base.

```
Gateway(config)#ip nat inside source list 1 interface serial 0
overload
```

Step 8. Specify the interfaces.

You must specify whether the active interfaces on the router are inside or outside interfaces with respect to PAT (NAT). To do this, use the ip nat inside or ip nat outside command.

```
Gateway(config)#interface fastethernet 0

Gateway(config-if)#ip nat inside

Gateway(config-if)#interface serial 0

Gateway(config-if)#ip nat outside
```

Step 9. Test the configuration.

A.   Configure a PC on the internal LAN with the IP address 10.10.10.10/24 and a default gateway 10.10.10.1. From the PCs, **ping** the Internet address 172.16.1.1. If successful, Telnet to the same IP address. Then look at the PAT translation on the gateway router by using the command **show ip nat translations**.

B.   What is the translation of the inside local host addresses?

_____ = _____ _____ = _____

C.   What does the number after the colon represent?

_____

D.   Why do all of the commands for PAT say NAT? _____

After you complete the previous steps, log off (by typing **exit**) and turn the router off. Then remove and store the cables and adapter.

Configuration Reference Sheet for This Lab

This sheet contains the basic configuration commands for the ISP and gateway routers.

ISP

```
Router#configure terminal
Router(config)#hostname ISP
ISP(config)#enable password cisco
ISP(config)#enable secret class
ISP(config)#line console 0
ISP(config-line)#password cisco
ISP(config-line)#login
ISP(config-line)#exit
ISP(config)#line vty 0 4
ISP(config-line)#password cisco
ISP(config-line)#login
ISP(config-line)#exit
ISP(config)#interface loopback 0
ISP(config-if)#ip address 172.16.1.1 255.255.255.255
ISP(config-if)#no shutdown
ISP(config-if)#exit
ISP(config)#interface serial 0
ISP(config-if)#ip address 200.2.2.17 255.255.255.252
ISP(config-if)#no shutdown
ISP(config-if)#clockrate 64000
ISP(config)#ip route 199.99.9.32 255.255.255.224 200.2.2.18
ISP(config)#end
ISP#copy running-config startup-config
```

Gateway

```
Router#configure terminal
Router(config)#hostname Gateway
Gateway(config)#enable password cisco
Gateway(config)#enable secret class
Gateway(config)#line console 0
Gateway(config-line)#password cisco
Gateway(config-line)#login
Gateway(config-line)#exit
Gateway(config)#line vty 0 4
Gateway(config-line)#password cisco
Gateway(config-line)#login
Gateway(config-line)#exit
Gateway(config)#interface fastethernet 0
Gateway(config-if)#ip address 10.10.10.1 255.255.255.0
Gateway(config-if)#no shutdown
Gateway(config-if)#exit
Gateway(config)#interface serial 0
Gateway(config-if)#ip address 200.2.2.18 255.255.255.252
Gateway(config-if)#no shutdown
Gateway(config)#ip route 0.0.0.0 0.0.0.0 200.2.2.17
Gateway(config)#end
Gateway#copy running-config startup-config
```

Lab 11-3   Configuring Static NAT Addresses (TI 1.1.4c)

Figure 11-3.1   Topology for Lab 11-3

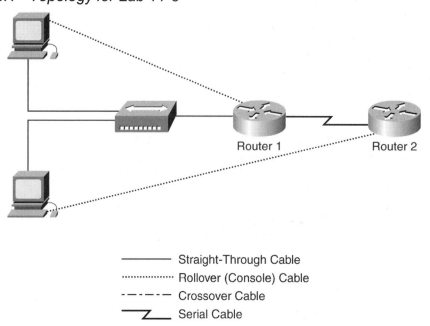

———— Straight-Through Cable
················· Rollover (Console) Cable
— · — · — Crossover Cable
——Z—— Serial Cable

Table 11-3.1 Lab Equipment Configuration

Router Designation	Router Name	Fast Ethernet 0 Address/ Subnet Mask	Interface Type	Serial 0 Address / Subnet Mask	Loopback 0 Address / Subnet Mask
Router 1	Gateway	10.10.10.1/24	DTE	200.2.2.18/30	NA
Router 2	ISP	NA	DCE	200.2.2.17/30	172.16.1.1/32

The enable secret password for both routers is **class**.
The enable, VTY, and console password for both routers is **cisco**.

Objectives

- Configure a router to use NAT to convert internal IP addresses, which are typically private addresses, into outside public addresses.

- Configure static IP mapping to allow outside access to an internal PC.

Background/Preparation

The ISP has allocated the public CIDR IP address 199.99.9.32/27 to a company. This is equivalent to 30 public IP addresses. Because the company has an internal requirement for more than 30 addresses, the IT manager has decided to use NAT. The company has decided to reserve the addresses 199.99.9.33 – 199.99.9.39 for static allocation and 199.99.9.40 – 199.99.9.62 for dynamic allocation. Routing between the ISP and the gateway router will be done by using a static route between the ISP and the gateway and a default route between the gateway and the ISP. The ISP connection to the Internet will be represented by a loopback address on the ISP router.

Cable a network that is similar to the one in Figure 11-3.1. You can use any router that meets the interface requirements that are displayed in the diagram (that is, 800, 1600, 1700, 2500, and 2600 routers or a combination). Please refer to the information in Appendix C to correctly specify the interface identifiers to be used based on the equipment in your lab. The configuration output used in this lab is produced from 1721 series routers. Another router might produce slightly different output. You should execute the following steps on each router unless you are specifically instructed otherwise. Start a HyperTerminal session.

Please refer to and implement the procedure documented in Appendix A before you continue with this lab.

Step 1. Configure the routers.

Configure the host name, console, virtual terminal and enable passwords, and the interfaces according to the chart. If you have trouble doing this, refer to the configuration reference sheet at the end of this lab.

Step 2. Save the configurations.

At the privileged EXEC mode prompt on both routers, type the command **copy running-config startup-config**.

Step 3. Configure the hosts with the proper IP address, subnet mask, and default gateway.

Each workstation should be able to **ping** the attached router. Troubleshoot as necessary. Hint: Remember to assign a specific IP address and default gateway to the workstation. If you are running Windows 98, check using **Start>Run>winipcfg**. If you are running Windows 2000 or later, check using **ipconfig** in a DOS window.

Step 4. Verify that the network is functioning.

    A.   From the attached hosts, **ping** the Fast Ethernet interface of the default gateway router.

    B.   Was the **ping** from the first host successful? _____

    C.   Was the **ping** from the second host successful? _____

    D.   If the answer is no for either question, troubleshoot the router and host configurations to find the error. Then **ping** again until they are successful.

Step 5. Create a static route.

    A.   Create a static route from the ISP to the gateway router. Addresses 199.99.9.32/27 have been allocated for Internet access outside the company. Use the **ip route** command to create the static route.

```
ISP(config)#ip route 199.99.9.32 255.255.255.224 200.2.2.18
```

    B.   Is the static route in the routing table?

          _____

C.   What command checks the routing table contents?

_____

D.   If the route was not in the routing table, give one reason why this might be so.

_____

Step 6. Create a default route.

A.   Add a default route, using the **ip route** command, from the gateway router to the ISP router. This forwards any unknown destination address traffic to the ISP.

```
Gateway(config)#ip route 0.0.0.0 0.0.0.0 200.2.2.17
```

B.   Is the route in the routing table? _____

C.   Try to **ping** from one of the workstations to the ISP serial interface IP address.

D.   Was the **ping** successful? _____

E.   Why?

_____

Step 7. Define the pool of usable public IP addresses.

To define the pool of public addresses, use the **ip nat pool** command.

```
Gateway(config)#ip nat pool public_access 199.99.9.40 199.99.9.62
netmask 255.255.255.224
```

Step 8. Define an Access List That Matches the Inside Private IP Addresses

To define the access list to match the inside private addresses, use the access list command.

```
Gateway(config)#access-list 1 permit 10.10.10.0 0.0.0.255
```

Step 9. Define the NAT translation from inside the list to outside the pool.

To define the NAT translation, use the ip nat inside source command.

```
Gateway(config)#ip nat inside source list 1 pool public_access
```

Step 10. Specify the interfaces.

You must specify whether the active interfaces on the router are inside or outside interfaces with respect to NAT. To do this, use either the **ip nat inside** or **ip nat outside** command.

Step 11. Configure static mapping.

A.   You should use workstation #1, 10.10.10.10/24, as the public WWW server. This server needs a permanent public IP address. Define this mapping by using a static NAT mapping.

B.   Configure one of the PCs on the LAN with the IP address 10.10.10.10/24 and a default gateway 10.10.10.1. To configure a static IP NAT mapping, use the **ip nat inside source static** command at the privileged EXEC mode prompt:

```
Gateway(config)#ip nat inside source static 10.10.10.10
199.99.9.33
```

This permanently maps 199.99.9.33 to the inside address 10.10.10.10.

C. Look at the translation table:

Gateway#**show ip nat translations**

Does the mapping show up in the output of the **show** command?

_____

Step 12. Test the configuration.

A. From the 10.10.10.10 workstation, **ping** 172.16.1.1.

B. Was the **ping** successful? _____

C. Why?

_____

D. From the ISP router, **ping** the host with the static NAT translation by typing **ping 10.10.10.10**.

E. What were the results of the **ping**? Was it successful?

_____

F. Why?

_____

G. From the ISP router, **ping** 199.99.9.33. If successful, look at the NAT translation on the gateway router by using the command **show ip nat translations**.

H. What is the translation of the inside local host addresses?

_____ = _____ _____ = _____

After you complete the previous steps, log off (by typing **exit**) and turn the router off. Then remove and store the cables and adapter.

Configuration Reference Sheet for This Lab

This sheet contains the basic configuration commands for the ISP and Gateway routers.

ISP

```
Router#configure terminal
Router(config)#hostname ISP
ISP(config)#enable password cisco
ISP(config)#enable secret class
ISP(config)#line console 0
ISP(config-line)#password cisco
ISP(config-line)#login
ISP(config-line)#exit
ISP(config)#line vty 0 4
ISP(config-line)#password cisco
ISP(config-line)#login
ISP(config-line)#exit
ISP(config)#interface loopback 0
ISP(config-if)#ip address 172.16.1.1 255.255.255.255
ISP(config-if)#no shutdown
ISP(config-if)#exit
ISP(config)#interface serial 0
```

```
ISP(config-if)#ip address 200.2.2.17 255.255.255.252
ISP(config-if)#no shutdown
ISP(config-if)#clockrate 64000
ISP(config)#ip route 199.99.9.32 255.255.255.224 200.2.2.18
ISP(config)#end
ISP#copy running-config startup-config
```

Gateway

```
Router#configure terminal
Router(config)#hostname Gateway
Gateway(config)#enable password cisco
Gateway(config)#enable secret class
Gateway(config)#line console 0
Gateway(config-line)#password cisco
Gateway(config-line)#login
Gateway(config-line)#exit
Gateway(config)#line vty 0 4
Gateway(config-line)#password cisco
Gateway(config-line)#login
Gateway(config-line)#exit
Gateway(config)#interface fastethernet 0
Gateway(config-if)#ip address 10.10.10.1 255.255.255.0
Gateway(config-if)#no shutdown
Gateway(config-if)#exit
Gateway(config)#interface serial 0
Gateway(config-if)#ip address 200.2.2.18 255.255.255.252
Gateway(config-if)#no shutdown
Gateway(config)#ip route 0.0.0.0 0.0.0.0 200.2.2.17
Gateway(config)#end
Gateway#copy running-config startup-config
```

Lab 11-4   Verifying NAT and PAT Configuration (TI 1.1.5)

Figure 11-4.1   Topology for Lab 11-4

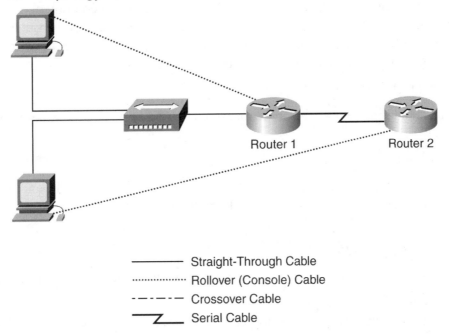

—————— Straight-Through Cable

···················· Rollover (Console) Cable

— · — · — · Crossover Cable

⎯⎯⎲⎯⎯ Serial Cable

Table 11-4.1 Lab Equipment Configuration

Router Designation	Router Name	Fast Ethernet 0 Address/ Subnet Mask	Interface Type	Serial 0 Address / Subnet Mask	Loopback 0 Address/ Subnet Mask
Router 1	Gateway	10.10.10.1/24	DTE	200.2.2.18/30	NA
Router 2	ISP	NA	DCE	200.2.2.17/30	172.16.1.1/32

The enable secret password for both routers is **class**.

The enable, VTY, and console password for both routers is **cisco**.

Objectives

- Configure a router for NAT and PAT.

- Test the configuration and verify NAT/PAT statistics.

Background/Preparation

The ISP has allocated the public CIDR IP address 199.99.9.32/30 to a company. This is equivalent to four public IP addresses. Because the company has an internal requirement for more than 30 addresses, the IT manager has decided to use NAT with PAT. Routing between the ISP and the gateway router will be done by using a static route between the ISP and the gateway and a default route between the gateway and the ISP. The ISP connection to the Internet will be represented by a loopback address on the ISP router.

Cable a network that is similar to the one in Figure 11-4.1. You can use any router that meets the interface requirements that are displayed in the diagram (that is, 800, 1600, 1700, 2500, and 2600 routers or a combination). Please refer to the information in Appendix C to correctly specify the interface identifiers to be used based on the equipment in your lab. The configuration output that is used in this lab is produced from 1721 series routers. Another router might produce slightly different output. You should execute the following steps on each router unless you are specifically instructed otherwise.

Start a HyperTerminal session.

Please refer to and implement the procedure documented in Appendix A before you continue with this lab.

Step 1. Configure the routers.

Configure the host name, console, virtual terminal and enable passwords, and the interfaces according to the chart. If you have trouble doing this, refer to Lab 11-1, "Configuring NAT (TI 1.1.4a)."

Step 2. Save the configurations.

At the privileged EXEC mode prompt on both routers, type the command **copy running-config startup-config**.

Step 3. Configure the hosts with the proper IP address, subnet mask, and default gateway.

Each workstation should be able to **ping** the attached router. Troubleshoot as necessary. Hint: Remember to assign a specific IP address and default gateway to the workstation. If you are running Windows 98, check using **Start>Run>winipcfg**. If you are running Windows 2000 or later, check using **ipconfig** in a DOS window.

Step 4. Verify that the network is functioning.

A.   From the attached hosts, **ping** the Fast Ethernet interface of the default gateway router.

B.   Was the **ping** from the first host successful? _____

C.   Was the **ping** from the second host successful? _____

D.   If the answer is no for either question, troubleshoot the router and host configurations to find the error. Then **ping** again until they are successful.

Step 5. Create a static route.

A.   Create a static route from the ISP to the gateway router. Addresses 199.99.9.32/30 have been allocated for Internet access outside of the company. Use the **ip route** command to create the static route.

```
ISP(config)#ip route 199.99.9.32 255.255.255.252 200.2.2.18
```

B.   Is the static route in the routing table? _____

C.   What command checks the routing table contents?
        _____

D.   If the route was not in the routing table, give one reason why this might be so.

Step 6. Create a default route.

    A.   Add a default route, using the **ip route** command, from the gateway router to the ISP router. This forwards any unknown destination address traffic to the ISP.

              `Gateway(config)#`**`ip route 0.0.0.0 0.0.0.0 200.2.2.17`**

    B.   Is the route in the routing table? _____

    C.   Try to **ping** from one of the workstations to the ISP serial interface IP address.

    D.   Was the **ping** successful? _____

    E.   Why?

              _____

Step 7. Define the pool of usable public IP addresses.

To define the pool of public addresses, use the **ip nat pool** command.

              `Gateway(config)#`**`ip nat pool public_access 199.99.9.32 199.99.9.35`**
              `netmask 255.255.255.252`

Step 8. Define an access list that matches the inside private IP addresses.

To define the access list to match the inside private addresses, use the access list command.

              `Gateway(config)#`**`access-list 1 permit 10.10.10.0 0.0.0.255`**

Step 9. Define the NAT translation from inside the list to outside the pool.

To define the NAT translation, use the ip nat inside source command.

              `Gateway(config)#`**`ip nat inside source list 1 pool public_access`**
              `overload`

Step 10. Specify the interfaces.

You must specify whether the active interfaces on the router are inside or outside interfaces with respect to NAT. To do this, use the ip nat inside or ip nat outside command.

              `Gateway(config)#`**`interface fastethernet 0`**

              `Gateway(config-if)#`**`ip nat inside`**

              `Gateway(config-if)#`**`interface serial 0`**

              `Gateway(config-if)#`**`ip nat outside`**

Step 11. Test the configuration.

    A.   From the workstations, **ping** 172.16.1.1. Open multiple DOS windows on each workstation and Telnet to the 172.16.1.1 address. Next, view the NAT translations on the gateway router with the command show ip nat translations.

    B.   What is the translation of the inside local host addresses?

              _____ = _____   _____ = _____

Step 12. Verify NAT/PAT statistics.

      A.   To view the NAT and PAT statistics, type the **show ip nat statistics** command at the privileged EXEC mode prompt.

      B.   How many active translations have taken place?

                _____

      C.   How many addresses are in the pool?

                _____

      D.   How many addresses have been allocated so far?

                _____

After you complete the previous steps, log off (by typing **exit**) and turn the router off. Then remove and store the cables and adapter.

Configuration Reference Sheet for This Lab

This sheet contains the basic configuration commands for the ISP and gateway routers.

ISP

```
Router#configure terminal
Router(config)#hostname ISP
ISP(config)#enable password cisco
ISP(config)#enable secret class
ISP(config)#line console 0
ISP(config-line)#password cisco
ISP(config-line)#login
ISP(config-line)#exit
ISP(config)#line vty 0 4
ISP(config-line)#password cisco
ISP(config-line)#login
ISP(config-line)#exit
ISP(config)#interface loopback 0
ISP(config-if)#ip address 172.16.1.1 255.255.255.255
ISP(config-if)#no shutdown
ISP(config-if)#exit
ISP(config)#interface serial 0
ISP(config-if)#ip address 200.2.2.17 255.255.255.252
ISP(config-if)#no shutdown
ISP(config-if)#clockrate 64000
ISP(config)#ip route 199.99.9.32 255.255.255.252 200.2.2.18
ISP(config)#end
ISP#copy running-config startup-config
```

Gateway

```
Router#configure terminal
Router(config)#hostname Gateway
Gateway(config)#enable password cisco
Gateway(config)#enable secret class
Gateway(config)#line console 0
Gateway(config-line)#password cisco
Gateway(config-line)#login
Gateway(config-line)#exit
Gateway(config)#line vty 0 4
```

```
Gateway(config-line)#password cisco
Gateway(config-line)#login
Gateway(config-line)#exit
Gateway(config)#interface fastethernet 0
Gateway(config-if)#ip address 10.10.10.1 255.255.255.0
Gateway(config-if)#no shutdown
Gateway(config-if)#exit
Gateway(config)#end
Gateway#copy running-config startup-config
Gateway(config)#interface serial 0
Gateway(config-if)#ip address 2.2.2.18 255.255.255.252
Gateway(config-if)#no shutdown
Gateway(config)#ip route 0.0.0.0 0.0.0.0 200.2.2.17
```

Lab 11-5   Troubleshooting NAT and PAT (TI 1.1.6)

Figure 11-5.1   Topology for Lab 11-5

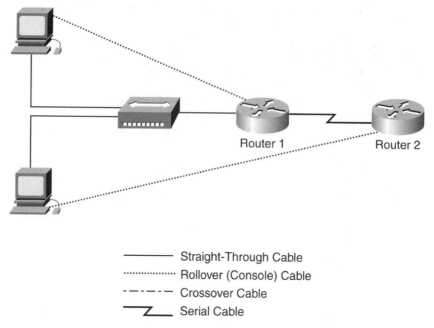

| Straight-Through Cable |
| Rollover (Console) Cable |
| Crossover Cable |
| Serial Cable |

Table 11-5.1 Lab Equipment Configuration

Router Designation	Router Name	Fast Ethernet 0 Address/ Subnet Mask	Interface Type	Serial 0 Address / Subnet Mask	Loopback 0 Address/ Subnet Mask
Router 1	Gateway	10.10.10.1/24	DTE	200.2.2.18/30	NA
Router 2	ISP	NA	DCE	200.2.2.17/30	172.16.1.1/32

The enable secret password for both routers is **class**.

The enable, VTY, and console password for both routers is **cisco**.

Objectives

- Configure a router for NAT and PAT.

- Troubleshoot NAT and PAT by using **debug**.

Background/Preparation

The ISP has allocated the public CIDR IP address 199.99.9.32/30 to a company. This is equivalent to four public IP addresses. Because the company has an internal requirement for more than 30 addresses, the IT manager has decided to use NAT and PAT. Routing between the ISP and the gateway router will be done by using a static route between the ISP and the gateway and a default route between the gateway and the ISP. The ISP's connection to the Internet will be represented by a loopback address on the ISP router.

Cable a network that is similar to the one in Figure 11-5.1. You can use any router that meets the interface requirements that are displayed in the diagram (that is, 800, 1600, 1700, 2500, and 2600 routers or a combination). Please refer to the information in Appendix C to correctly specify the interface identifiers to be used based on the equipment in your lab. The configuration output used in this lab is produced from 1721 series routers. Another router might produce slightly different output. You should execute the following steps on each router unless you are specifically instructed otherwise.

Start a HyperTerminal session.

Refer to the erase and reload instructions at the end of this lab. Perform those steps on all routers in this lab assignment before you continue.

Step 1. Configure the routers.

Configure the host name, console, virtual terminal and enable passwords, and the interfaces according to the chart. If you have trouble doing this, refer to Lab 11-1, "Configuring NAT (TI 1.1.4a)."

Step 2. Save the configurations.

At the privileged EXEC mode prompt on both routers, type the command **copy running-config startup-config**.

Step 3. Configure the hosts with the proper IP address, subnet mask, and default gateway.

Each workstation should be able to **ping** the attached router. Troubleshoot as necessary. Hint: Remember to assign a specific IP address and default gateway to the workstation. If you are running Windows 98, check using **Start>Run>winipcfg**. If you are running Windows 2000 or later, check using **ipconfig** in a DOS window.

Step 4. Verify that the network is functioning.

    A.   From the attached hosts, **ping** the Fast Ethernet interface of the default gateway router.

    B.   Was the **ping** from the first host successful? _____

    C.   Was the **ping** from the second host successful? _____

    D.   If the answer is no for either question, troubleshoot the router and host configurations to find the error. Then **ping** again until they are successful.

Step 5. Create a static route.

    A.   Create a static route from the ISP to the gateway router. Addresses 199.99.9.32/30 have been allocated for Internet access outside the company. Use the **ip route** command to create the static route.

```
ISP(config)#ip route 199.99.9.32 255.255.255.252 200.2.2.18
```

    B.   Is the static route in the routing table? _____

    C.   What command checks the routing table contents?

        _____

    D.   If the route was not in the routing table, give one reason why this might be so.

Step 6. Create a default route.

    A.   Add a default route, using the **ip route** command, from the gateway router to the ISP router. This forwards any unknown destination address traffic to the ISP.

```
Gateway(config)#ip route 0.0.0.0 0.0.0.0 200.2.2.17
```

    B.   Is the route in the routing table? _____

    C.   Try to **ping** from one of the workstations to the ISP serial interface IP address.

    D.   Was the **ping** successful? _____

    E.   Why?

_____

Step 7. Define the pool of usable public IP addresses.

To define the pool of public addresses, use the **ip nat pool** command.

```
Gateway(config)#ip nat pool public_access 199.99.9.32 199.99.9.35
netmask 255.255.255.252
```

Step 8. Define an access list that matches the inside private IP addresses.

To define the access list to match the inside private addresses, use the access list command.

```
Gateway(config)#access-list 1 permit 10.10.10.0 0.0.0.255
```

Step 9. Define the NAT translation from inside the list to outside the pool.

To define the NAT translation, use the ip nat inside source command.

```
Gateway(config)#ip nat inside source list 1 pool public_access
overload
```

Step 10. Specify the interfaces.

You must specify whether the active interfaces on the router are inside or outside interfaces with respect to NAT. To do this, use the ip nat inside command.

```
Gateway(config)#interface fastethernet 0
```

```
Gateway(config-if)#ip nat inside
```

Step 11. Test the configuration.

    A.   Turn on debugging for the NAT process by typing **debug ip nat** at the privileged EXEC mode prompt.

    B.   Does the **debug** command show output? _____

    C.   If translation was taking place, there would be output from the debug command. In reviewing the running configuration of the gateway router, you see that the **ip nat outside** statement has not been entered on the serial 0 interface. To configure this, enter the following:

```
Gateway(config)#interface serial 0
```

```
Gateway(config-if)#ip nat outside
```

D.   From the workstations, **ping** 172.16.1.1.

If you entered the **ip nat outside** statement correctly, there should be output from the **debug ip nat** command.

E.   What does the NAT*: S=10.10.10.? -> 199.99.9 mean?

_____

F.   To stop the debug output, type **undebug all** at the privileged EXEC mode prompt.

After you complete the previous steps, log off (by typing **exit**) and turn the router off. Then remove and store the cables and adapter.

Configuration Reference Sheet for This Lab

This sheet contains the basic configuration commands for the ISP and gateway routers.

ISP

```
Router#configure terminal
Router(config)#hostname ISP
ISP(config)#enable password cisco
ISP(config)#enable secret class
ISP(config)#line console 0
ISP(config-line)#password cisco
ISP(config-line)#login
ISP(config-line)#exit
ISP(config)#line vty 0 4
ISP(config-line)#password cisco
ISP(config-line)#login
ISP(config-line)#exit
ISP(config)#interface loopback 0
ISP(config-if)#ip add 172.16.1.1 255.255.255.255
ISP(config-if)#no shutdown
ISP(config-if)#exit
ISP(config)#interface serial 0
ISP(config-if)#ip add 200.2.2.17 255.255.255.252
ISP(config-if)#no shutdown
ISP(config-if)#clockrate 64000
ISP(config)#ip route 199.99.9.32 255.255.255.252 200.2.2.18
ISP(config)#end
ISP#copy running-config startup-config
Destination filename [startup-config]?[Enter]
```

Gateway

```
Router#configure terminal
Router(config)#hostname Gateway
Gateway(config)#enable password cisco
Gateway(config)#enable secret class
Gateway(config)#line console 0
Gateway(config-line)#password cisco
Gateway(config-line)#login
Gateway(config-line)#exit
Gateway(config)#line vty 0 4
Gateway(config-line)#password cisco
Gateway(config-line)#login
```

```
Gateway(config-line)#exit
Gateway(config)#interface fastethernet 0
Gateway(config-if)#ip add 10.10.10.1 255.255.255.0
Gateway(config-if)#no shutdown
Gateway(config-if)#exit
Gateway(config)#end
Gateway#copy running-config startup-config
Gateway(config)#interface serial 0
Gateway(config-if)#ip add 200.2.2.18 255.255.255.252
Gateway(config-if)#no shutdown
Gateway(config)#ip route 0.0.0.0 0.0.0.0 200.2.2.17
```

Lab 11-6   Configuring DHCP (TI 1.2.6)

Figure 11-6-1   Topology for Lab 11-6

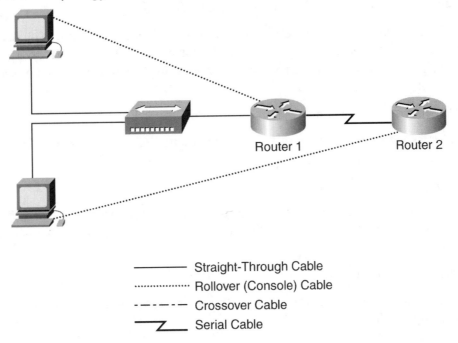

——————— Straight-Through Cable

·················· Rollover (Console) Cable

— — — — Crossover Cable

⌐Z⌐ Serial Cable

Table 11-6.1 Lab Equipment Configuration

Router Designation	Router Name	Fast Ethernet 0 Address/ Subnet Mask	Interface Type	Serial 0 Address / Subnet Mask	Loopback 0 Address/ Subnet Mask
Router 1	campus	172.16.12.1/24	DCE	172.16.1.6/30	NA
Router 2	ISP	NA	DTE	172.16.1.5/30	172.16.13.1/32

The enable secret password for both routers is **class**.

The enable, VTY, and console password for both routers is **cisco**.

Objective

Configure a router for DHCP to dynamically assign addresses to attached hosts.

Background/Preparation

Routing between the ISP and the campus router is by way of a static route between the ISP and the gateway and a default route between the gateway and the ISP. The ISP connection to the Internet is identified by a loopback address on the ISP router.

Cable a network that is similar to the one in Figure 11-6.1. You can use any router that meets the interface requirements displayed in the diagram (that is, 800, 1600, 1700, 2500, and 2600 routers or a combination, with some exceptions). Please refer to the information in Appendix

C to correctly specify the interface identifiers to be used based on the equipment in your lab. The configuration output used in this lab is produced from 1721 series routers. Another router might produce slightly different output. You should execute the following steps on each router unless you are specifically instructed otherwise.

Note: Before beginning this lab, verify that the routers being used support DHCP. Some IOS versions for the 1600 and 2500 series routers do not support DHCP services. Type **ip ?** at the global configuration prompt to verify that the **dhcp** option "Configure DHCP server and relay parameters" is available.

Start a HyperTerminal session.

Please refer to and implement the procedure documented in Appendix A before you continue with this lab.

Step 1. Configure the routers.

Configure the host name, console, virtual terminal and enable passwords, and the interfaces according to the chart. If you have trouble doing this, refer to Lab 11-1, "Configuring NAT (TI 1.1.4a)."

Step 2. Save the configurations.

At the privileged EXEC mode prompt on both routers, type the command **copy running-config startup-config**.

Step 3. Create a static route.

    A.   Addresses 172.16.12.0/24 have been allocated for Internet access outside the company. Use the **ip route** command to create the static route.

```
ISP(config)#ip route 172.16.12.0 255.255.255.0 172.16.1.6
```

    B.   Is the static route in the routing table? _____

Step 4. Create a default route.

    A.   Use the **ip route** command to add a default route from the campus router to the ISP router. This provides the mechanism to forward unknown destination address traffic to the ISP.

```
campus(config)#ip route 0.0.0.0 0.0.0.0 172.16.1.5
```

    B.   Is the route in the routing table? _____

Step 5. Create the DHCP address pool.

To configure the campus LAN pool, use the following commands:

```
campus(config)#ip dhcp pool campus
campus(dhcp-config)#network 172.16.12.0 255.255.255.0
campus(dhcp-config)#default-router 172.16.12.1
campus(dhcp-config)#dns-server 172.16.1.2
campus(dhcp-config)#domain-name foo.com
campus(dhcp-config)#netbios-name-server 172.16.1.10
```

Step 6. Exclude addresses from the pool.

To exclude addresses from the pool, use the following commands:

```
campus(dhcp-config)#ip dhcp excluded-address 172.16.12.1 172.16.12.10
```

Step 7. Verify DHCP operation.

A.   At each workstation on the directly connected subnet, configure the TCP/IP properties so that the workstation obtains an IP address and DNS server address from the DHCP server (see Figure 11-6.2). After you change and save the configuration, reboot the workstation.

Figure 11-6.2   TCP/IP Properties Dialog Box

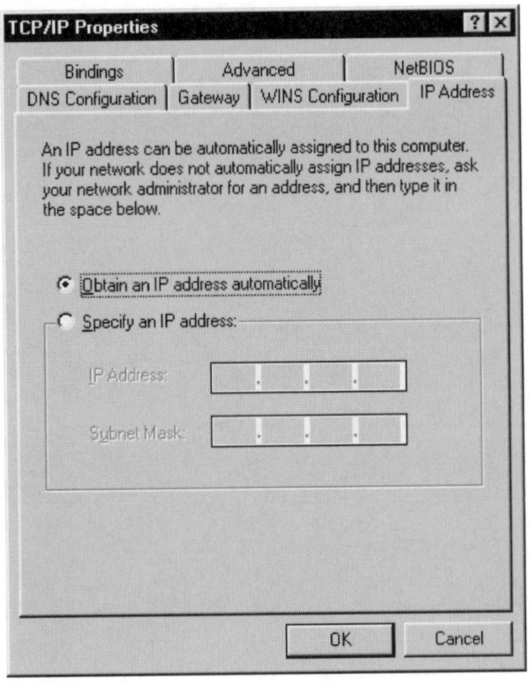

B.   To confirm the TCP/IP configuration information on each host, use **Start>Run>winipcfg**. If you are running Windows 2000, check using **ipconfig** in a DOS window.

C.   What IP address was assigned to the workstation?

_____

D.   What other information was assigned automatically?

_____   _____   _____

E.   When was the lease obtained?

_____

F.   When will the lease expire?

_____

Step 8. View DHCP bindings.

    A.   From the campus router, you can see the bindings for the hosts. To see the bindings, use the command **show ip dhcp binding** at the privileged EXEC mode prompt.

    B.   What IP addresses were assigned? _____ _____

    C.   What three other fields are listed in the output?

        _____ _____ _____

After you complete the previous steps, log off (by typing **exit**) and turn the router off. Then remove and store the cables and adapter.

Lab 11-7 Configuring DHCP Relay (TI 1.2.8)

Figure 11-7-1 Topology for Lab 11-7 (?? In diag, JL

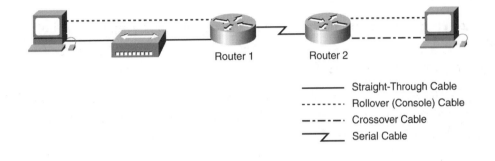

Router 1   Router 2

———— Straight-Through Cable
-------- Rollover (Console) Cable
—·—·—· Crossover Cable
⎯z⎯ Serial Cable

Table 11-7-1 Lab Equipment Configuration

Router Designation	Router Name	Fast Ethernet 0 Address/ Subnet Mask	Interface Type	Serial 0 Address
Router 1	campus	172.16.12.1/24	DCE	172.16.1.6/30
Router 2	remote	172.16.13.1/24	DTE	172.16.1.5/30

The enable secret password for both routers is **class**.
The enable, VTY, and console password for both routers is **cisco**.

Objectives

- Configure a router for DHCP.

- Add the capability for workstations to remotely obtain DHCP addresses and dynamically assign addresses to the attached hosts.

Background/Preparation

A DHCP client uses IP broadcasts to find the DHCP server. However, routers do not forward these broadcasts, so in the case of the remote LAN, the workstations cannot locate the DHCP server. The router must be configured with the **ip helper-address** command to enable forwarding of these broadcasts, as unicast packets, to the specific server.

Routing between the remote and the campus router is done by using a static route between remote and gateway and a default route between gateway and remote.

Cable a network that is similar to the one in Figure 11-7.1. You can use any router that meets the interface requirements displayed in the diagram (that is, 800, 1600, 1700, 2500, and 2600 routers or a combination, with some exceptions). Please refer to the information in Appendix C to correctly specify the interface identifiers to be used based on the equipment in your lab. The configuration output used in this lab is produced from 1721 series routers. Another router might produce slightly different output. You should execute the following steps on each router unless you are specifically instructed otherwise.

Note: Before beginning this lab, verify that the routers being used support DHCP. Some IOS versions for the 1600 and 2500 series routers do not support DHCP services. Type **ip ?** at the global configuration prompt to verify that the **dhcp** option "Configure DHCP server and relay parameters" is available.

Start a HyperTerminal session.

Please refer to and implement the procedure documented in Appendix A before you continue with this lab.

Step 1. Configure the routers.

Configure the host name, console, virtual terminal and enable passwords, and the interfaces according to the chart. If you have a problem completing this, refer to Lab 11-1, "Configuring NAT (TI 1.1.4a)."

Step 2. Configure routing on the remote router.

Using OSPF as the routing protocol, set up the network as area 0 and the process ID as 1.

```
remote(config)#router ospf 1
remote(config-router)#network 172.16.1.0 0.0.0.255 area 0
remote(config-router)#network 172.16.13.0 0.0.0.255 area 0
```

Step 3. Configure routing on the campus router.

    A.   Using OSPF as the routing protocol, set up the network as area 0 and the process ID as 1.

```
campus(config)#router ospf 1
campus(config-router)#network 172.16.1.0 0.0.0.255 area 0
campus(config-router)#network 172.16.12.0 0.0.0.255 area 0
```

    B.   Do OSPF routes exist in the routing table? _____

Step 4. Save the configurations.

At the privileged EXEC mode prompt on both routers, type the command **copy running-config startup-config**.

Step 5. Create the campus DHCP address pool on the campus router.

To configure the campus LAN pool, use the following commands:

```
campus(config)#ip dhcp pool campus
campus(dhcp-config)#network 172.16.12.0 255.255.255.0
campus(dhcp-config)#default-router 172.16.12.1
campus(dhcp-config)#dns-server 172.16.12.2
campus(dhcp-config)#domain-name foo.com
campus(dhcp-config)#netbios-name-server 172.16.12.10
```

Step 6. Create the remote DHCP address pool on the campus router.

To configure the remote LAN pool, use the following commands:

```
campus(dhcp-config)#ip dhcp pool remote
campus(dhcp-config)#network 172.16.13.0 255.255.255.0
campus(dhcp-config)#default-router 172.16.13.1
campus(dhcp-config)#dns-server 172.16.12.2
campus(dhcp-config)#domain-name foo.com
campus(dhcp-config)#netbios-name-server 172.16.12.10
```

Step 7. Exclude addresses from the pool.

   A.   To exclude addresses from the pool, use the following commands:

```
campus(dhcp-config)#ip dhcp excluded-address 172.16.12.1
172.16.12.10

campus(dhcp-config)#ip dhcp excluded-address 172.16.13.1
172.16.13.10
```

This defines the address range that the DHCP server excludes from dynamic issue.

   B.   Why would addresses be excluded? _____

Step 8. Verify DHCP operation on the campus router.

   A.   From the workstation that is directly connected to the campus router, configure the TCP/IP properties for the workstation to obtain its IP properties automatically from DHCP. These properties include the IP and DNS server address (see Figure 11-7.2).

Figure 11-7.2   TCP/IP Properties Dialog Box

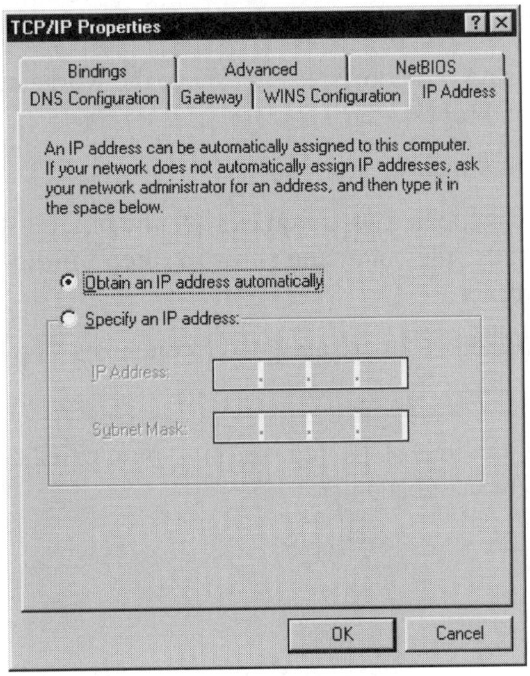

   B.   After you change the configuration, reboot the workstation. View the TCP/IP configuration information on each host. If you are running Windows 98, go to **Start>Run>winipcfg**. With Windows 2000 or higher, use **ipconfig** in a DOS command prompt window.

   C.   What IP address was assigned to the workstation? _____

Step 9. Verify DHCP operation on the remote router.

    A.   Repeat the last step using the workstation that is attached to the remote router.

    B.   Is there a valid address assigned from the DHCP pool? _____

    C.   What IP address was assigned to the workstation? _____

    D.   What does this address (if any) represent?

Step 10. Configure DHCP relay.

Configure the remote router with the **ip helper-address** command to enable forwarding of broadcasts, as unicast packets, to the specific server. You must configure this command on the LAN interface of the remote router for DHCP to function.

```
remote(config)#interface fastethernet 0
remote(config-if)#ip helper-address 172.16.12.1
```

Step 11. Verify DHCP operation on the remote router.

    A.   Reboot the workstation that is attached to the remote router.

    B.   Is a valid address assigned from the DHCP pool? _____

    C.   What IP address was assigned to the workstation? _____

    D.   If there is no IP address, troubleshoot the workstation and router configurations and repeat step 11.

Step 12. View DHCP bindings.

    A.   From the campus router, you can see the bindings for the hosts. To see the bindings, use the command **show ip dhcp binding** at the privileged EXEC mode prompt.

    B.   Which IP addresses are assigned to the hosts?

        _____ _____

After you complete the previous steps, log off (by typing **exit**) and turn the router off. Then remove and store the cables and adapter.

CCNA 4

Chapter 12: WAN Technologies

There are no hands-on labs associated with the topic of this chapter. Please review the information in Chapter 12 of the *Cisco Networking Academy Program CCNA 3 and 4 Companion Guide* to ensure that you can do the following:

- Understand the differences between a LAN and WAN

- Identify the devices used in a WAN

- List WAN standards

- Describe WAN encapsulation

- Classify the various WAN link options

- Differentiate between packet-switched and circuit-switched WAN technologies

- Describe the steps in WAN design

CCNA 4

Chapter 13: Point-to-Point Protocol

The following table maps the numbering scheme that is used in this chapter's labs to the Target Indicators (TIs) that are used in the online curriculum.

Lab Companion Numbering	Online Curriculum TI
Lab 13-1	3.1.7
Lab 13-2	3.3.2
Lab 13-3	3.3.3
Lab 13-4	3.3.4
Lab 13-5	3.3.5

Lab 13-1 Troubleshooting a Serial Interface (TI 3.1.7)

Figure 13-1.1 Topology for Lab 13-1

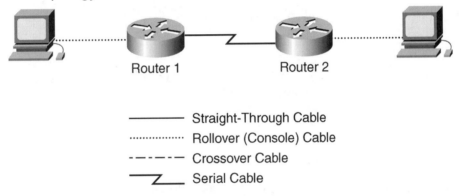

Router 1   Router 2

————— Straight-Through Cable
·············· Rollover (Console) Cable
– – – – – Crossover Cable
—Z— Serial Cable

Table 13-1.1 Lab Equipment Configuration

Router Designation	Router Name	Interface Type	Serial 0 Address
Router 1	London	DCE	192.168.15.1
Router 2	Paris	DTE	192.168.15.2

The enable secret password for both routers is **class**.

The enable, VTY, and console password for both routers is **cisco**.

The subnet mask for both routers is 255.255.255.0.

Objectives

÷ Configure a serial interface on two routers.

÷ Use **show** commands to troubleshoot connectivity issues.

Background/Preparation

Cable a network that is similar to the one in Figure 13-1.1. You can use any router that meets the interface requirements in Figure 13-1.1 (that is, 800, 1600, 1700, 2500, and 2600 routers or a combination). Refer to the information in Appendix C, "Router Interface Summary Chart," to correctly specify the interface identifiers based on the equipment in your lab. The 1721 series routers produced the configuration output in this lab. Another router might produce slightly different output. You should execute the following steps on each router unless you are specifically instructed otherwise. Start a HyperTerminal session.

Implement the procedure documented in Appendix A, "Erasing and Reloading the Router," on all routers before you continue with this lab.

Step 1. Configure the routers.

Configure the host name, console, vty, and enable passwords according to Table 13-1.1. If you have difficulty doing this, refer to Lab 11-1, "Configuring NAT (TI 1.1.4a)."

Step 2. Configure the Paris interface as shown.

Configure the Paris router serial interface as follows:

```
Paris(config)#interface serial 0
Paris(config-if)#ip address 192.168.15.2 255.255.255.0
Paris(config-if)#clockrate 56000
Paris(config-if)#no shutdown
Paris(config-if)#exit
Paris(config)#exit
```

Step 3. Configure the London interface as shown.

Configure the London router serial interface as follows:

```
London(config)#interface serial 0
London(config-if)#ip address 192.168.15.1 255.255.255.0
London(config-if)#no shutdown
London(config-if)#exit
London(config)#exit
```

Step 4. Save the configuration.

```
London#copy running-config startup-config

Paris#copy running-config startup-config
```

Step 5. Enter the command **show interface serial 0** (refer to Appendix C) on London.

```
London#show interface serial 0
```

This shows the details of interface serial 0.

Answer the following questions:

    A.   Serial 0 is _____, and line protocol is_____.

    B.   What type of problem is indicated in the last statement?

         _____

         _____

    C.   Internet address is _____.

    D.   Encapsulation _____.

Step 6. Enter the command **show interface serial 0** (refer to Appendix C) on Paris.

       `Paris#`**`show interface serial 0`**

This shows the details of interface serial 0.

Answer the following questions.

    A.   Serial 0 is _____, and line protocol is_____.

    B.   Internet address is _____.

    C.   Encapsulation _____.

    D.   To what OSI layer is the "Encapsulation" referring? _____

    E.   Why is the interface down?

         _____

Step 7. Correct the clock location.

The clock rate statement has been placed on the wrong interface. It is currently placed on the Paris router, but the London router is the DCE. Remove the clock rate statement from the Paris router by using the NO version of the command. Then add it to the London router's configuration.

Step 8. Enter the command **show interface serial 0** on Paris.

       `Paris#`**`show interface serial 0`**

    A.   Serial0 is _____, and line protocol is_____.

    B.   What is the difference in the Line and Protocol status that was recorded on Paris earlier? Why?

         _____

Step 9. Verify that the serial connection is functioning by **ping**ing the serial interface of the other router.

       `London#`**`ping 192.168.15.2`**

       `Paris#`**`ping 192.168.15.1`**

    A.   From London, can you **ping** the Paris router's serial interface? _____

B.   From Paris, can you **ping** the London router's serial interface? _____

C.   If the answer is no for either question, troubleshoot the router configurations to find the error. Then do the **ping**s again until the answer to both questions is yes.

After you complete the previous steps, log off (by typing **exit**) and turn the router off. Then remove and store the cables and adapter.

Lab 13-2 Configuring PPP Encapsulation (TI 3.3.2)

Figure 13-2.1 Topology for Lab 13-2

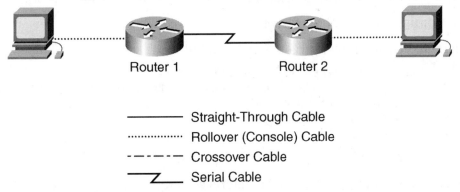

Router 1   Router 2

——————— Straight-Through Cable
················· Rollover (Console) Cable
— — - — — Crossover Cable
——Z—— Serial Cable

Table 13-2.1 Lab Equipment Configuration

Router Designation	Router Name	Interface Type	Serial 0 Address
Router 1	Washington	DCE	192.168.15.1
Router 2	Dublin	DTE	192.168.15.2

The enable secret password for both routers is **class**.

The enable, VTY, and console password for both routers is **cisco**.

The subnet mask for both routers is 255.255.255.0.

Objectives

÷ Configure the serial interfaces on two routers with the PPP protocol.

÷ Test the link for connectivity.

Background/Preparation

Cable a network that is similar to the one in Figure 13-2.1. You can use any router that meets the interface requirements in Figure 13-2.1 (that is, 800, 1600, 1700, 2500, and 2600 routers or a combination). Refer to the information in Appendix C to correctly specify the interface identifiers based on the equipment in your lab. The 1721 series routers produced the configuration output in this lab. Another router might produce slightly different output. You should execute the following steps on each router unless you are specifically instructed otherwise. Start a HyperTerminal session.

Implement the procedure documented in Appendix A on all routers before you continue with this lab.

Step 1. Configure the routers.

Configure the host name, console, VTY, and enable passwords according to Table 13-2.1. If you have difficulty doing this, refer to Lab 11-1, "Configuring NAT (TI 1.1.4a)."

Step 2. Configure the Dublin interface as shown.

Configure the Dublin router serial interface as follows:

```
Dublin(config)#interface serial 0
Dublin(config-if)#ip address 192.168.15.2 255.255.255.0
Dublin(config-if)#no shutdown
Dublin(config-if)#exit
Dublin(config)#exit
```

Step 3. Configure the Washington interface as shown.

Configure the Washington router serial interface as follows:

```
Washington(config)#interface serial 0
Washington(config-if)#ip address 192.168.15.1 255.255.255.0
Washington(config-if)#clockrate 64000
Washington(config-if)#no shutdown
Washington(config-if)#exit
Washington(config)#exit
```

Step 4. Save the configuration.

```
Washington#copy running-config startup-config
```

```
Dublin#copy running-config startup-config
```

Step 5. Enter the command **show interface serial 0** (refer to Appendix C) on Washington.

```
Washington#show interface serial 0
```

A.   This shows the details of interface serial 0.

B.   Serial 0 is _____, and line protocol is_____.

C.   Internet address is _____.

D.   Encapsulation _____.

Step 6. Enter the command **show interface serial 0** (refer to Appendix C) on Dublin.

```
Dublin#show interface serial 0
```

A.   This shows the details of interface serial 0.

B.   Serial 0 is _____, and line protocol is_____.

C.   Internet address is _____.

D.   Encapsulation _____.

Step 7. Change the encapsulation type.

Change the encapsulation type to PPP by typing **encapsulation ppp** at the interface serial 0 configuration mode prompt on both routers.

```
Washington(config-if)#encapsulation ppp
Dublin(config-if)#encapsulation ppp
```

Step 8. Enter the command **show interface serial 0** on Washington.

```
Washington#show interface serial 0
```

Encapsulation _____

Step 9. Enter the command **show interface serial 0** on Dublin.

```
Dublin#show interface serial 0
```

Encapsulation _____

Step 10. Verify that the serial connection is functioning by **ping**ing the serial interface of the other router.

```
Washington#ping 192.168.15.2
```

```
Dublin#ping 192.168.15.1
```

A.   From Washington, can you **ping** the Dublin router's serial interface?

_____

B.   From Dublin, can you **ping** the Washington router's serial interface?

_____

C.   If the answer is no for either question, troubleshoot the router configurations to find the error. Then do the **ping**s again until the answer to both questions is yes.

After you complete the previous steps, log off (by typing **exit**) and turn the router off. Then remove and store the cables and adapter.

Lab 13-3 Configuring PPP Authentication (TI 3.3.3)

Figure 13-3.1 Topology for Lab 13-3

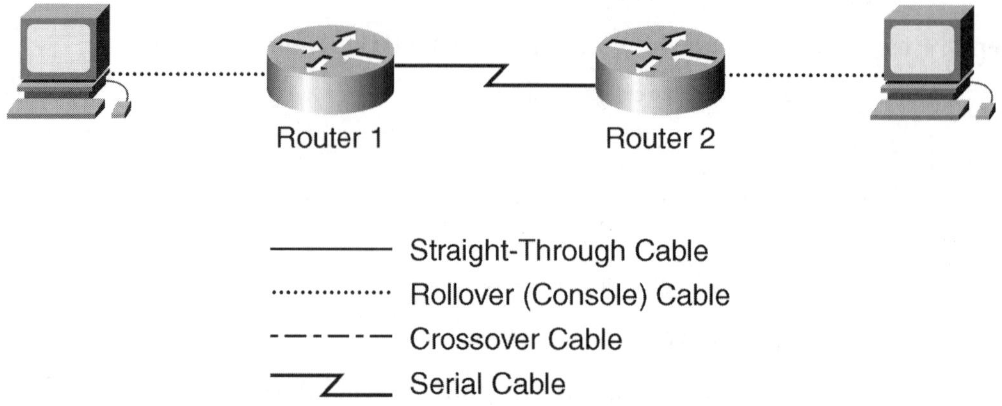
Router 1
Router 2
Straight-Through Cable
Rollover (Console) Cable
Crossover Cable
Serial Cable

Table 13-3.1 Lab Equipment Configuration

Router Designation	Router Name	Interface Type	Serial 0 Address
Router 1	Madrid	DCE	192.168.15.1
Router 2	Tokyo	DTE	192.168.15.2

The enable secret password for both routers is **class**.

The enable, VTY, and console password for both routers is **cisco**.

The subnet mask for both routers is 255.255.255.0.

Objective

Configure a PPP authentication by using CHAP on two routers.

Background/Preparation

Cable a network that is similar to the one in Figure 13-3.1. You can use any router that meets the interface requirements in Figure 13-3-1 (that is, 800, 1600, 1700, 2500, and 2600 routers or a combination). Refer to the information in Appendix C to correctly specify the interface identifiers based on the equipment in your lab. The 1721 series routers produced the configuration output in this lab. Another router might produce slightly different output. You should execute the following steps on each router unless you are specifically instructed otherwise. Start a HyperTerminal session.

Implement the procedure documented in Appendix A on all routers before you continue with this lab.

Step 1. Configure the routers.

Configure the host name, console, VTY, and enable passwords according to Table 13-3.1. If you have difficulty doing this, refer to Lab 11-1, "Configuring NAT (TI 1.1.4a)."

Step 2. Configure the Tokyo interface as shown.

Configure the Tokyo router serial interface as follows:

```
Tokyo(config)#interface serial 0
Tokyo(config-if)#ip address 192.168.15.2 255.255.255.0
Tokyo(config-if)#encapsulation ppp
Tokyo(config-if)#no shutdown
Tokyo(config-if)#exit
Tokyo(config)#exit
```

Step 3. Configure the Madrid interface as shown.

Configure the Madrid router serial interface as follows:

```
Madrid(config)#interface serial 0
Madrid(config-if)#ip address 192.168.15.1 255.255.255.0
Madrid(config-if)#clockrate 64000
Madrid(config-if)#encapsulation ppp
Madrid(config-if)#no shutdown
Madrid(config-if)#exit
Madrid(config)#exit
```

Step 4. Save the configuration.

```
Madrid#copy running-config startup-config
Tokyo#copy running-config startup-config
```

Step 5. Enter the command **show interface serial 0** on Madrid.

```
Madrid#show interface serial 0
```

Encapsulation _____.

Step 6. Enter the command **show interface serial 0** on Tokyo.

```
Tokyo#show interface serial 0
```

Encapsulation _____.

Step 7. Verify that the serial connection is functioning by **ping**ing the serial interface of the other router.

```
Madrid#ping 192.168.15.2
```

```
Tokyo#ping 192.168.15.1
```

If the **ping**s are unsuccessful, troubleshoot the router configurations to find the error. Then do the **ping**s again until both **ping**s are successful.

Step 8. Configure PPP authentication.

Configure usernames and passwords on the Madrid router. The passwords must be the same on both routers. The username must reflect the other router's host name exactly. (It is case sensitive.)

```
Madrid(config)#username Tokyo password cisco
Madrid(config)#interface serial 0
```

```
Madrid(config-if)#ppp authentication chap
```

Step 9. Verify that the serial connection is functioning.

A.   Verify that the serial connection is functioning by **ping**ing the serial interface of the other router.

```
Madrid#ping 192.168.15.2
```

B.   Was the **ping** successful? _____

C.   Why?

_____

Step 10. Configure PPP authentication.

Configure usernames and passwords on the Tokyo router. The passwords must be the same on both routers. The usernames must reflect the other router's host name exactly (case sensitive).

```
Tokyo(config)#username Madrid password cisco
Tokyo(config)#interface serial 0
Tokyo(config-if)#ppp authentication chap
```

Step 11. Verify that the serial connection is functioning.

A.   Verify that the serial connection is functioning by **ping**ing the serial interface of the other router.

```
Tokyo#ping 192.168.15.1
```

B.   Was the **ping** successful? _____

C.   Why?

_____

After you complete the previous steps, log off (by typing **exit**) and turn the router off. Then remove and store the cables and adapter.

Lab 13-4 Verifying PPP Configuration (TI 3.3.4)

Figure 13-4.1 Topology for Lab 13-4

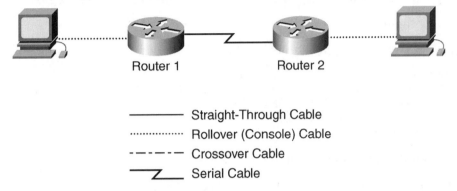

Router 1   Router 2

———— Straight-Through Cable

·············· Rollover (Console) Cable

– — – — – Crossover Cable

—⌐—— Serial Cable

Table 13-4.1 Lab Equipment Configuration

Router Designation	Router Name	Interface Type	Serial 0 Address
Router 1	Brasilia	DCE	192.168.15.1
Router 2	Warsaw	DTE	192.168.15.2

The enable secret password for both routers is **class**.

The enable, VTY, and console password for both routers is **cisco**.

The subnet mask for both routers is 255.255.255.0.

Objectives

÷ Configure a serial interface on two routers with the PPP protocol.

÷ Verify and test the link for connectivity.

Background/Preparation

Cable a network that is similar to the one in Figure 13-4.1. You can use any router that meets the interface requirements in Figure 13-4-1 (that is, 800, 1600, 1700, 2500, and 2600 routers or a combination). Refer to the information in Appendix C to correctly specify the interface identifiers based on the equipment in your lab. The 1721 series routers produced the configuration output in this lab. Another router might produce slightly different output. You should execute the following steps on each router unless you are specifically instructed otherwise. Start a HyperTerminal session.

Implement the procedure documented in Appendix A on all routers before you continue with this lab.

Step 1. Configure the routers.

Configure the host name, console, VTY, and enable passwords according to Table 13-4.1. If you have difficulty doing this, refer to Lab 11-1, "Configuring NAT (TI 1.1.4a)."

Step 2. Configure the Warsaw interface as shown.

Configure the Warsaw router serial interface as follows:

```
Warsaw(config)#interface serial 0
Warsaw(config-if)#ip address 192.168.15.2 255.255.255.0
Warsaw(config-if)#no shutdown
Warsaw(config-if)#exit
Warsaw(config)#exit
```

Step 3. Configure the Brasilia interface as shown.

Configure the Brasilia router serial interface as follows:

```
Brasilia(config)#interface serial 0
Brasilia(config-if)#ip address 192.168.15.1 255.255.255.0
Brasilia(config-if)#clockrate 64000
Brasilia(config-if)#no shutdown
Brasilia(config-if)#exit
Brasilia(config)#exit
```

Step 4. Save the configuration.

```
Brasilia#copy running-config startup-config

Warsaw#copy running-config startup-config
```

Step 5. Enter the command **show interface serial 0** (refer to Appendix C) on Brasilia.

```
Brasilia#show interface serial 0
```

This shows the details of interface serial 0.

Encapsulation _____.

Step 6. Enter the command **show interface serial 0** (refer to Appendix C) on Warsaw.

```
Warsaw#show interface serial 0
```

This shows the details of interface serial 0.

Encapsulation _____.

Step 7. Turn on PPP debugging.

Turn on the PPP debug function on both routers by typing **debug ppp tasks** at the privileged EXEC mode prompt. Note: For some routers and IOS versions, it may be necessary to use the command **debug ppp events**.

Step 8. Change the encapsulation type.

A.   Change the encapsulation type to PPP by typing **encapsulation ppp** at the interface serial 0 configuration mode prompt on both routers.

```
Brasilia(config-if)#encapsulation ppp

Warsaw(config-if)#encapsulation ppp
```

B.   What did the debug function report when the PPP encapsulation was applied to each router?

_____

C.   Turn off the debug function by typing **undebug all** at the privileged EXEC mode prompt.

Step 9. Enter the command **show interface serial 0** on Brasilia.

```
Brasilia#show interface serial 0
```

Encapsulation _____.

Step 10. Enter the command **show interface serial 0** on Warsaw.

```
Warsaw#show interface serial 0
```

Encapsulation _____.

Step 11. Verify that the serial connection is functioning.

A.   **Ping** the other router to verify that there is connectivity between the two routers.

```
Brasilia#ping 192.168.15.2
```

```
Warsaw#ping 192.168.15.1
```

B.   From Brasilia, can you **ping** the Warsaw router's serial interface? _____

C.   From Warsaw, can you **ping** the Brasilia router's serial interface? _____

D.   If the answer is no for either question, troubleshoot the router configurations to find the error. Then do the **ping**s again until the answer to both questions is yes.

After you complete the previous steps, log off (by typing **exit**) and turn the router off. Then remove and store the cables and adapter.

Lab 13-5 Troubleshooting PPP Configuration (TI 3.3.5)

Figure 13-5.1 Topology for Lab 13-5

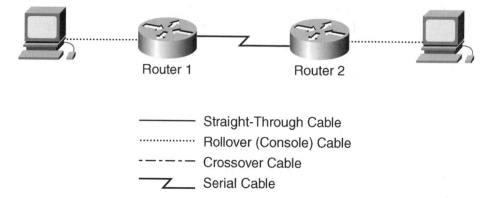

Router 1   Router 2

——— Straight-Through Cable
·············· Rollover (Console) Cable
– – – – – Crossover Cable
⎯⎯z⎯⎯ Serial Cable

Table 13-5.1 Lab Equipment Configuration

Router Designation	Router Name	Interface Type	Serial 0 Address
Router 1	London	DCE	192.168.15.1
Router 2	Paris	DTE	192.168.15.2

The enable secret password for both routers is **class**.

The enable, VTY, and console password for both routers is **cisco**.

The subnet mask for both routers is 255.255.255.0.

Objectives

÷ Configure a PPP on the serial interfaces of two routers.

÷ Use **show** and **debug** commands to troubleshoot connectivity issues.

Background/Preparation

Cable a network that is similar to the one in Figure 13-5.1. You can use any router that meets the interface requirements in Figure 13-5.1 (that is, 800, 1600, 1700, 2500, and 2600 routers or a combination). Refer to the information in Appendix C to correctly specify the interface identifiers based on the equipment in your lab. The 1721 series routers produced the configuration output in this lab. Another router might produce slightly different output. You should execute the following steps on each router unless you are specifically instructed otherwise. Start a HyperTerminal session.

Implement the procedure documented in Appendix A on all routers before you continue with this lab.

Step 1. Configure the routers.

Configure the host name, console, vty, and enable passwords according to Table 13-5.1. If you have difficulty doing this, refer to Lab 11-1, "Configuring NAT (TI 1.1.4a)."

Step 2. Configure the Paris interface as shown.

Configure the Paris router serial interface as follows:

```
Paris(config)#interface serial 0
Paris(config-if)#ip address 192.168.15.2 255.255.255.0
Paris(config-if)#clockrate 56000
Paris(config-if)#no shutdown
Paris(config-if)#exit
Paris(config)#exit
```

Step 3. Configure the London interface as shown.

Configure the London router serial interface as follows:

```
London(config)#interface serial 0
London(config-if)#ip address 192.168.15.1 255.255.255.0
London(config-if)#encapsulation ppp
London(config-if)#no shutdown
London(config-if)#exit
London(config)#exit
```

Step 4. Save the configuration.

```
London#copy running-config startup-config
Paris#copy running-config startup-config
```

Step 5. Enter the command **show interface serial 0** (refer to Appendix C) on London.

```
London#show interface serial 0
```

This shows the details of interface serial 0.

A.   List the following information discovered from issuing this command.

B.   Serial 0 is _____, and line protocol is_____.

C.   What type of problem is indicated in the last statement?

_____

_____

D.   Internet address is _____.

E.   Encapsulation _____.

Step 6. Enter the command **show interface serial 0** (refer to Appendix C) on Paris.

```
Paris#show interface serial 0
```

This shows the details of interface serial 0.

A.   List the following information discovered from issuing this command.

B.   Serial 0 is _____, and line protocol is_____.

C.   Internet address is _____.

D.   Encapsulation _____.

E. To what OSI layer is the "Encapsulation" referring? _____

F. If the Serial interface was configured, why did the **show interface serial 0** output show that the interface is down?

_____

Step 7. Correct the clock location.

The **clock rate** statement has been placed on the wrong interface. It is currently placed on the Paris router, but the London router is the DCE. Remove the **clock rate** statement from the Paris router by using the **no** version of the command and then add it to the configuration for the London router.

Step 8. Enter the command **show cdp neighbors** on London.

A. Is there output from the command? _____

B. Should there be output? _____

Step 9. Enter the command **debug ppp negotiation** on London.

It might take 60 seconds or more before output occurs.

A. Is there output? _____

B. What is the output saying?

_____

C. Is there a problem with PPP encapsulation on the London router or the Paris router? _____

D. Why?

E. What were the encapsulations listed for the interfaces?

London? _____ Paris? _____

F. Is there an issue with the preceding statement? _____

G. What is the issue?

_____

Step 10. Enter the command **debug ppp negotiation** on Paris.

A. Enter the command **debug ppp negotiation** on the Paris router at the privileged EXEC mode prompt.

B. Is there output from the **debug** command? _____

Step 11. Correct the encapsulation type.

A. Convert the encapsulation to PPP on the Paris router.

B. Is there output from the **debug** command? _____

C. Does it confirm link establishment? _____

Step 12. Enter the command **show interface serial 0** on Paris.

```
Paris#show interface serial 0
```

A.   Serial0 is _____, and line protocol is_____.

B.   Encapsulation _____.

C.   What is the difference between the Line and Protocol status recorded on Paris earlier? Why?

_____

Step 13. Verify that the serial connection is functioning by **ping**ing the serial interface of the other router.

```
London#ping 192.168.15.1
```

```
Paris#ping 192.168.15.2
```

A.   From London, can you **ping** the serial interface on the Paris router? _____

B.   From Paris, can you **ping** the serial interface on the London router? _____

C.   If the answer is no for either question, troubleshoot the router configurations to find the error. Then do the **ping**s again until the answer to both questions is yes.

After you complete the previous steps, log off (by typing **exit**) and turn the router off. Then remove and store the cables and adapter.

CCNA 4

Chapter 14: ISDN and DDR

The following table maps the numbering scheme that is used in this chapter's labs to the Target Indicators (TIs) that are used in the online curriculum.

Lab Companion Numbering	Online Curriculum TI
Lab 14-1	4.2.1
Lab 14-2	4.3.2
Lab 14-3	4.3.7

Lab 14-1 Configuring ISDN BRI (U-Interface) (TI 4.2.1)

Figure 14-1.1 Topology for Lab 14-1

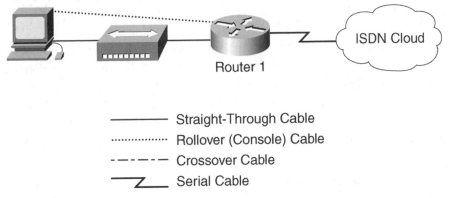

Table 14-1.1 Lab Equipment Configuration

Router Designation	Router Name	Fast Ethernet0 Address/Subnet Mask	BRI 0 Address	Adtran Connection
Router 1	Ottawa	192.168.14.1/24	N/A	BRI 1

The enable secret password for this router is **class**.

The enable, VTY, and console password for this router is **cisco**.

Objective

Configure an ISDN router to make a successful connection to a local ISDN switch.

Background/Preparation

This lab assumes that a router with an ISDN BRI U interface is available. An Adtran Atlas550 ISDN emulator is used to simulate the ISDN switch and cloud. If an ISDN router is not available, review the lab and perform as many non-interface commands as possible.

Cable a network that is similar to the one in Figure 14-1.1. You can use any router that meets the interface requirements in Figure 14-1.1 (that is, 800, 1600, 1700, 2500, and 2600 routers or a combination). Refer to the information in Appendix C, "Router Interface Summary Chart," to correctly specify the interface identifiers based on the equipment in your lab. The 1721 series routers produced the configuration output in this lab. Another router might produce slightly different output. You should execute the following steps on each router unless you are specifically instructed otherwise. Start a HyperTerminal session.

Implement the procedure documented in Appendix A, "Erasing and Reloading the Router," on all routers before you continue with this lab.

Step 1. Configure the router.

Configure the host name, console, VTY, and enable passwords according to Table 14-1.1.

Step 2. Verify the ISDN BRI switch type.

A.   Not all ISDN switch types are the same worldwide, and the first step is to configure the ISDN TE1 device (the router) to tell it what ISDN switch type is in use. The ISDN telco provider will provide this information. In this case, the ISDN switch type, which the Adtran simulator supports, is National ISDN-1 (North America) and is configured on the router using the keyword **basic-ni**. To check the ISDN BRI status, issue the following command before you issue configuration commands:

```
Ottawa#show isdn status
```

B.   What is the Layer 1 status?

_____

C.   What is the ISDN switch type?

_____

Step 3. Specify the switch type.

A.   To specify the ISDN switch type, use the **isdn switch-type** command at the global configuration mode prompt. You can review the different switch types that are available by using the **isdn switch-type ?** command.

```
Ottawa#configure terminal
Ottawa(config)#isdn switch-type ?
```

B.   How many different switch types are available? _____

C.   To configure the router to communicate with a National ISDN-1 switch type:

```
Ottawa(config)#isdn switch-type basic-ni
```

Step 4. Verify the switch status.

    A.   Check the state of the ISDN interface again.

```
Ottawa#show isdn status
```

    B.   What is the Layer 1 status?

    _____

    C.   What is the ISDN switch type?

    _____

Step 5. Activate the BRI connection.

Activate the ISDN BRI by using the **no shutdown** command at the interface configuration prompt.

```
Ottawa#configure terminal
Ottawa(config)#interface bri 0
Ottawa(config-if)#no shutdown
```

Step 6. Review the switch status.

    A.   At this stage, the ISDN BRI should be physically active and one TEI should be negotiated. Enter the following command to review the switch status:

```
Ottawa#show isdn status
```

    B.   What is the Layer 1 status?

    _____

    C.   What is the ISDN switch type?

    _____

    D.   Has the Layer 2 status changed? _____

Step 7. Configure the ISDN SPIDs.

Depending on the region, you might have to specify ISDN Service Profile Identifiers (SPIDs) for the ISDN switch to respond to the ISDN TE1 correctly. The SPIDs that the Adtran simulator supports are specified as **isdn spid1** and **isdn spid2**. To configure the SPIDs, issue the following commands:

```
Ottawa(config)#interface bri 0
Ottawa(config-if)#isdn spid1 51055510000001 5551000
Ottawa(config-if)#isdn spid2 51055510010001 5551001
```

Step 8. Review the switch status

    A.   Check the state of the ISDN interface again.

```
Ottawa#show isdn status
```

    B.   What does the output specify about SPID1?

    _____

C.   What does the output specify about SPID2?

_____

D.   If you examine this output carefully, you will see that the assigned SPID values have not been sent to the ISDN switch and have not been verified. This is because you specified them after the ISDN interface was enabled. To send the SPID values, you must reset the interface.

Step 9. Reset the interface.

A.   To manually reset the ISDN BRI interface, issue the command **clear interface bri 0**. This causes all ISDN parameters to be renegotiated. Issue the **clear** command on the router, and then check the ISDN interface status. SPID1 and SPID2 will be sent and validated.

```
Ottawa#clear interface bri 0
Ottawa#show isdn status
```

B.   Have SPID1 and SPID2 been sent and verified? _____

Step 10. Save the configuration and reboot.

A.   Save the configuration and reboot the router. This time, verify that the ISDN Interface has correctly negotiated with the ISDN switch. Review activity on the ISDN interface by using the **show isdn active** command.

```
Ottawa#copy running-config startup-config
Ottawa#reload
```

```
Ottawa#show isdn active
```

B.   The history table has a maximum of how many entries? _____

C.   The history table data is retained for how long? _____

After you complete the previous steps, log off (by typing **exit**) and turn the router off. Then remove and store the cables and adapter.

Lab 14-2   Configuring Legacy DDR (TI 4.3.2)

Figure 14-2.1   Topology for Lab 14-2

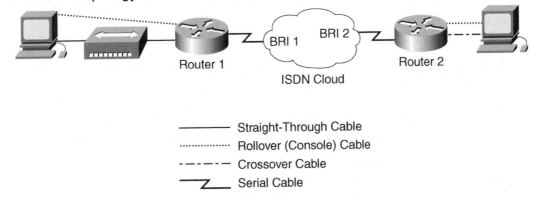

————— Straight-Through Cable

··············· Rollover (Console) Cable

— — — — Crossover Cable

⌐——Z— Serial Cable

Table 14-2.1 Lab Equipment Configuration

Router Designation	Router Name	Fast Ethernet0 Address/Subnet Mask	SPID Numbers	Phone Numbers	Adtran Connection
Router 1	Tokyo	192.168.1.1/24	51055510000001	5551000	BRI 1
			51055510010001	5551001	
Router 2	Moscow	192.168.2.1/24	51055520000001	5552000	BRI 2
			51055520010001	5552001	

The enable secret password for both routers is **class**.

The enable, VTY, and console password for both routers is **cisco**.

Objectives

÷   Configure an ISDN router to make a Legacy DDR call to another ISDN-capable router.

÷   When the DDR connection is made successfully, augment the configuration to specify that only HTTP traffic will bring up the link.

Background/Preparation

In this lab, two ISDN routers are required. If ISDN routers are not available, review the lab to become familiar with the process. An Adtran Atlas550 ISDN emulator is used to simulate the switch/ISDN cloud.

Cable a network that is similar to the one in Figure 14-2.1. You can use any router that meets the interface requirements in Figure 14-2.1 (that is, 800, 1600, 1700, 2500, and 2600 routers or a combination). Refer to the information in Appendix C to correctly specify the interface identifiers based on the equipment in your lab. The 1721 series routers produced the configuration output in this lab. Another router might produce slightly different output. You should execute the following steps on each router unless you are specifically instructed otherwise. Start a HyperTerminal session.

Implement the procedure documented in Appendix A on all routers before you continue with this lab.

Step 1. Configure the router.

Configure the host name, console, VTY, and enable passwords according to Table 14-2.1. If you have difficulty doing this, refer to Lab 11-1, "Configuring NAT (TI 1.1.4a)."

Step 2. Define the switch type and SPID numbers.

You must specify the switch type and SPID numbers on the routers:

```
Router(config)#hostname Tokyo
Tokyo(config)#enable secret class
Tokyo(config)#isdn switch-type basic-ni
Tokyo(config)#interface fastethernet 0
Tokyo(config-if)#ip address 192.168.1.1 255.255.255.0
Tokyo(config-if)#no shutdown
Tokyo(config-if)#exit
Tokyo(config)#interface bri 0
Tokyo(config-if)#isdn spid1 51055510000001 5551000
Tokyo(config-if)#isdn spid2 51055510010001 5551001
Tokyo(config-if)#no shutdown

Router(config)# hostname Moscow
Moscow(config)# enable secret class
Moscow(config)# isdn switch-type basic-ni
Moscow(config)# interface fastethernet 0
Moscow(config-if)#ip address 192.168.2.1 255.255.255.0
Moscow(config-if)#no shutdown
Moscow(config-if)#exit
Moscow(config)# interface bri 0
Moscow(config-if)#isdn spid1 51055520000001 5552000
Moscow(config-if)#isdn spid2 51055520010001 5552001
Moscow(config-if)#no shutdown
```

Step 3. Define the static routes for DDR.

A.   Use static and default routes instead of dynamic routing so that you can reduce the cost of the dialup connection. To configure a static route, you must know the network address of the network to be reached as well as the IP address of the next router on the path to this destination.

```
Moscow#configure terminal
```

```
Moscow(config)# ip route 192.168.1.0 255.255.255.0 192.168.3.1
```

```
Tokyo#configure terminal
```

```
Tokyo(config)# ip route 0.0.0.0 0.0.0.0 192.168.3.2
```

B.   Execute the **show ip route** command to verify that the routes exist.

Step 4. Specify interesting traffic for DDR.

Specify the traffic that will cause the DDR interface to dial up the remote router. For the moment, declare that all IP traffic is "interesting." You do this by using the **dialer-list** command.

```
Tokyo#configure terminal
Tokyo(config)#dialer-list 1 protocol ip permit
Tokyo(config)#interface bri 0
Tokyo(config-if)#dialer-group 1
Tokyo(config-if)#end
```

Step 5. Configure the DDR dialer information for router 1.

A. Configure the correct dialer information that is necessary for the correct function of the dialer profile and dialer interface. This includes IP address information, PPP configuration, name, passwords, and dial number.

```
Tokyo#configure terminal
Tokyo(config)#interface bri 0
Tokyo(config-if)#ip address 192.168.3.1 255.255.255.0
```

B. Configure the PPP information.

```
Tokyo#configure terminal
Tokyo(config)#username Moscow password class
Tokyo(config)#interface bri 0
Tokyo(config-if)#encapsulation ppp
Tokyo(config-if)#ppp authentication chap
```

C. Configure the dial information.

```
Tokyo#configure terminal
Tokyo(config)#interface bri 0
Tokyo(config-if)#dialer idle-timeout 120
Tokyo(config-if)#dialer map ip 192.168.3.2 name Moscow 5552000
```

Step 6. Configure the DDR dialer information for router 2.

```
Moscow#configure terminal
Moscow(config)# dialer-list 1 protocol ip permit
Moscow(config)# username Tokyo password class
Moscow(config)# interface bri 0
Moscow(config-if)#ip address 192.168.3.2 255.255.255.0
Moscow(config-if)#dialer-group 1
Moscow(config-if)#encapsulation ppp
Moscow(config-if)#ppp authentication chap
```

```
Moscow(config-if)#dialer idle-timeout 120
Moscow(config-if)#dialer map ip 192.168.3.1 name Tokyo 5551000
```

Step 7. View the Tokyo router configuration.

    A.   To view the configuration, use the **show running-config** command.

```
Tokyo#show running-config
```

    B.   What authentication is being used?

_____

    C.   What are the dialer strings on the Tokyo router?

_____

Step 8. Verify the DDR configuration.

    A.   Generate some interesting traffic across the DDR link from the remote Moscow router to verify that connections are made correctly and that the dialer profiles are functioning.

```
Tokyo#ping 192.168.2.1
```

    B.   Were the **ping**s successful?

_____

    C.   If not, troubleshoot the router configuration.

    D.   Use the **show dialer** command to show the reason for the call. This information is shown for each channel.

```
Tokyo#show dialer
```

    E.   Which dialer strings are associated with Dialer1 ? __

    F.   What is the last status for dial string 5552000 in the Dialer1 readout? ____

    G.   Use the **show interface** command and note that the output shows that the interface is "spoofing." This provides a mechanism for the interface to simulate an active state for internal processes, such as routing, on the router. You can also use the **show interface** command to display information about the B channel.

```
Tokyo#show interface bri 0
```

After you complete the previous steps, log off (by typing **exit**) and turn the router off. Then remove and store the cables and adapter.

Lab 14-3 Configuring Dialer Profiles (TI 4.3.7)

Figure 14-3.1 Topology for Lab 14-3

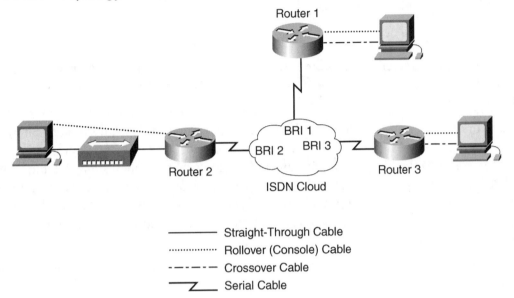

```
                        Router 1

              BRI 1
        BRI 2      BRI 3
Router 2                      Router 3
        ISDN Cloud
```

───────── Straight-Through Cable

·············· Rollover (Console) Cable

─ ─ ─ ─ ─ Crossover Cable

──╱── Serial Cable

Table 14-3.1 Lab Equipment Configuration

Router Designation	Router Name	Fast Ethernet0 Address with Subnet Mask	SPID Numbers	Phone Numbers	Adtran Connection
Router 1	Tokyo	192.168.1.1/24	51055510000001 51055510010001	5551000 5551001	BRI 1
Router 2	Moscow	192.168.2.1/24	51055520000001 51055520010001	5552000 5552001	BRI 2
Router 3	Sydney	192.168.3.1/24	51055530000001 51055530010001	5553000 5553001	BRI 3

The enable secret password for all routers is **class**.

The enable, VTY, and console password for all routers is **cisco**.

Objective

Configure ISDN dialer profiles on the routers, enabling a DDR call to be made from two remote routers simultaneously into a central ISDN BRI router.

Background/Preparation

In this lab, three ISDN routers are required. If ISDN routers are not available, review the lab to become familiar with the process. An Adtran Atlas550 ISDN emulator is used to simulate the switch/ISDN cloud.

Cable a network that is similar to the one in Figure 14-3.1. You can use any router that meets the interface requirements in Figure 14-3.1 (that is, 800, 1600, 1700, 2500, and 2600 routers or a combination). Refer to the information in Appendix C to correctly specify the interface identifiers based on the equipment in your lab. The 1721 series routers produced the configuration output in this lab. Another router might produce slightly different output. You should execute the following steps on each router unless you are specifically instructed otherwise. Start a HyperTerminal session.

Implement the procedure documented in Appendix A on all routers before you continue with this lab.

Step 1. Configure the router.

Configure the host name, console, VTY, and enable passwords according to Table 14-3.1. If you have difficulty doing this, refer to Lab 11-1, "Configuring NAT (TI 1.1.4a)."

Step 2. Define the switch type and SPID numbers.

To configure the switch type and SPID numbers, use the following commands:

```
Router(config)#hostname Tokyo
Tokyo(config)#enable secret class
Tokyo(config)#isdn switch-type basic-ni
Tokyo(config)#interface fastethernet 0
Tokyo(config-if)#ip address 192.168.1.1 255.255.255.0
Tokyo(config-if)#no shutdown
Tokyo(config-if)#exit
Tokyo(config)#interface bri 0
Tokyo(config-if)#isdn spid1 51055510000001 5551000
Tokyo(config-if)#isdn spid2 51055510010001 5551001
Tokyo(config-if)#no shutdown

Router(config)#hostname Moscow
Moscow(config)#enable secret class
Moscow(config)#isdn switch-type basic-ni
Moscow(config)#interface fastethernet 0
Moscow(config-if)#ip address 192.168.2.1 255.255.255.0
Moscow(config-if)#no shutdown
Moscow(config-if)#exit
Moscow(config)#interface bri 0
Moscow(config-if)#isdn spid1 51055520000001 5552000
Moscow(config-if)#isdn spid2 51055520010001 5552001
Moscow(config-if)#no shutdown
```

```
Router(config)#hostname Sydney
Sydney(config)#enable secret class
Sydney(config)#isdn switch-type basic-ni
Sydney(config)#interface fastethernet 0
Sydney(config-if)#ip address 192.168.3.1 255.255.255.0
Sydney(config-if)#no shutdown
Sydney(config-if)#exit
Sydney(config)#interface bri 0
Sydney(config-if)#isdn spid1 51055530000001 5553000
Sydney(config-if)#isdn spid2 51055530010001 5553001
Sydney(config-if)#no shutdown
```

Step 3. Define the static routes for DDR.

Use static and default routes instead of dynamic routing so that you can reduce the cost of the dialup connection. To configure a static route, you must know the network address of the network trying to be reached as well as the IP address of the next router on the path to this destination.

```
Moscow#configure terminal

Moscow(config)#ip route 0.0.0.0 0.0.0.0 192.168.253.1


Sydney#configure terminal
Sydney(config)#ip route 0.0.0.0 0.0.0.0 192.168.254.1


Tokyo#configure terminal
Tokyo(config)#ip route 192.168.2.0 255.255.255.0 192.168.253.2
Tokyo(config)#ip route 192.168.3.0 255.255.255.0 192.168.254.2
```

Step 4. Specify interesting traffic for DDR.

You must define traffic as "interesting" to cause the DDR interface to dial up the remote router. For the moment, declare that all IP traffic is interesting by using the **dialer-list** command.

```
Moscow(config)#dialer-list 1 protocol ip permit
Moscow(config)#interface dialer 0
Moscow(config-if)#dialer-group 1

Sydney(config)#dialer-list 1 protocol ip permit
Sydney(config)#interface dialer 0
Sydney(config-if)#dialer-group 1

Tokyo#configure terminal
Tokyo(config)#dialer-list 1 protocol ip permit
Tokyo(config)#interface dialer 1
Tokyo(config-if)#description The Profile for the Moscow router
Tokyo(config-if)#dialer-group 1
Tokyo(config-if)#interface dialer 2
Tokyo(config-if)#description The Profile for the Sydney router
Tokyo(config-if)#dialer-group 1
```

Step 5. Configure the DDR dialer information.

Configure the correct dialer information that is necessary for the correct function of the dialer profile and dialer interface. This includes IP address information, PPP configuration, name, passwords, and dial number.

```
Tokyo(config)#interface dialer 1
Tokyo(config-if)#ip address 192.168.253.1 255.255.255.0
Tokyo(config-if)#interface dialer 2
Tokyo(config-if)#ip address 192.168.254.1 255.255.255.0
Tokyo(config-if)#interface bri 0
Tokyo(config-if)#encapsulation ppp
Tokyo(config-if)#ppp authentication chap
Tokyo(config-if)#interface dialer 1
Tokyo(config-if)#encapsulation ppp
Tokyo(config-if)#ppp authentication chap
Tokyo(config-if)#interface dialer 2
Tokyo(config-if)#encapsulation ppp
Tokyo(config-if)#ppp authentication chap
Tokyo(config-if)#exit
Tokyo(config)#username Moscow password class
Tokyo(config)#username Sydney password class

Moscow(config)#interface dialer 0
Moscow(config-if)#ip address 192.168.253.2 255.255.255.0
Moscow(config-if)#interface bri 0
Moscow(config-if)#encapsulation ppp
Moscow(config-if)#ppp authentication chap
Moscow(config-if)#interface dialer 0
Moscow(config-if)#encapsulation ppp
Moscow(config-if)#ppp authentication chap
Moscow(config-if)#no shutdown
Moscow(config-if)#exit
Moscow(config)#username Tokyo password class

Sydney(config)#interface dialer 0
Sydney(config-if)#ip address 192.168.254.2 255.255.255.0
Sydney(config-if)#interface bri 0
Sydney(config-if)#encapsulation ppp
Sydney(config-if)#ppp authentication chap
Sydney(config-if)#interface dialer 0
Sydney(config-if)#encapsulation ppp
Sydney(config-if)#ppp authentication chap
Sydney(config-if)#no shutdown
Sydney(config-if)#exit
Sydney(config)#username Tokyo password class
```

Step 6. Configure the dialer information.

Next, you must configure the dial information to specify the remote name of the remote router in the dialer profile, as well as the dial string (phone number) to use to contact this remote device. Use the following commands to do this:

A.   To configure the dial information on Tokyo, use the following:

```
Tokyo(config)#interface dialer 1
Tokyo(config-if)#dialer remote-name Moscow
Tokyo(config-if)#dialer string 5552000
Tokyo(config-if)#dialer string 5552001
Tokyo(config-if)#interface dialer 2
Tokyo(config-if)#dialer remote-name Sydney
Tokyo(config-if)#dialer string 5553000
Tokyo(config-if)#dialer string 5553001
```

B.   To configure the dial information on Moscow, use the following:

```
Moscow(config-if)#interface dialer 0
Moscow(config-if)#dialer remote-name Tokyo
Moscow(config-if)#dialer string 5551000
Moscow(config-if)#dialer string 5551001
```

C.   To configure the dial information on Sydney, use the following:

```
Sydney(config-if)#interface dialer 0
Sydney(config-if)#dialer remote-name Tokyo
Sydney(config-if)#dialer string 5551000
Sydney(config-if)#dialer string 5551001
```

Step 7. Associate the dialer profiles.

Finally, associate the dialer profiles with the dialer interfaces that will be used, when needed. Create a dialer pool, and put the interfaces and the associated dialer profiles in a common pool. The commands for doing this are as follows.

A.   On Tokyo, the commands issued would be as follows:

```
Tokyo(config-if)#interface bri 0
Tokyo(config-if)#dialer pool-member 1
Tokyo(config-if)#interface dialer 1
Tokyo(config-if)#dialer pool 1

Tokyo(config-if)#interface dialer 2

Tokyo(config-if)#dialer pool 1
```

B.   On Moscow, the commands issued would be as follows:

```
Moscow(config-if)#interface bri 0
Moscow(config-if)#dialer pool-member 1
Moscow(config-if)#interface dialer 0
Moscow(config-if)#dialer pool 1
```

C.   Use the same commands to configure the Sydney router.

Step 8. Configure the dialer timeouts.

    A.   Configure a **dialer idle-timeout** of 60 seconds for each of the dialer interfaces.

```
Tokyo(config)# interface dialer 1
Tokyo(config-if)#dialer idle-timeout 60
Tokyo(config-if)#interface dialer 2
Tokyo(config-if)#dialer idle-timeout 60
```

    B.   Repeat these commands on Moscow and Sydney.

Step 9. View the Tokyo router configuration.

    A.   To view the configuration, use the **show running-config** command.

```
Tokyo#show running-config
```

    B.   How many username statements exist? _____

    C.   What authentication type is being used for PPP?

        _____

    D.   Which sections of the configuration list the authentication type?

        _____

    E.   What are the dialer strings on the Tokyo router?

        _____

Step 10. Verify the DDR configuration.

    A.   Generate some interesting traffic across the DDR link from Moscow and Sydney to verify that connections are made correctly and that the dialer profiles are functioning.

```
Moscow#ping 192.168.1.1
```

    B.   Were the **ping**s successful? _____

    C.   If not, troubleshoot the router configurations.

    D.   What other information was displayed when the **ping** was issued?

        _____

```
Sydney#ping 192.168.1.1
```

    E.   Were the **ping**s successful? _____

    F.   If not, troubleshoot the router configurations.

    G.   Use the **show dialer** command to see the reason for the call. This information is shown for each channel.

```
Tokyo#show dialer
```

    H.   Which dialer strings are associated with Dialer1?___

I.   What is the last status for dial string 5553000 in the Dialer2 readout? _____

J.   Use the **show interface** command and note that the output shows that the interface is "spoofing." This provides a mechanism for the interface to simulate an active state for internal processes, such as routing, on the router. You can also use the **show interface** command to display information about the B channel.

```
Tokyo#show interface bri 0
```

After you complete the previous steps, log off (by typing **exit**) and turn the router off. Then remove and store the cables and adapter.

CCNA 4

Chapter 15: Frame Relay

The following table maps the numbering scheme that is used in this chapter's labs to the Target Indicators (TIs) that are used in the online curriculum.

Lab Companion Numbering	Online Curriculum TI
Lab 15-1	5.2.1
Lab 15-2	5.2.2
Lab 15-3	5.2.5
Lab 15-4	No corresponding online lab

Lab 15-1   Configuring Frame Relay (TI 5.2.1)

Figure 15-1.1   Topology for Lab 15-1

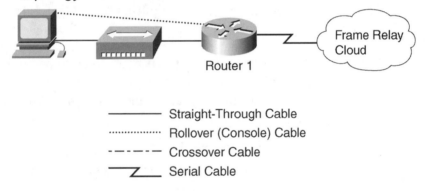

Router 1

———— Straight-Through Cable
·············· Rollover (Console) Cable
– – – – – Crossover Cable
——Z—— Serial Cable

Table 15-1.1 Lab Equipment Configuration

Router Designation	Router Name	Fast Ethernet 0 Address/Subnet Mask	Adtran Connection
Router 1	Cork	192.168.14.1/24	1/1

The enable secret password for this router is **class**.

The enable, VTY, and console password for this router is **cisco**.

Objective

Configure a router to establish a connection to a local Frame Relay switch.

Background/Preparation

This lab uses an Adtran Atlas550 Frame Relay to simulate the Frame Relay switch/cloud.

The Cork Wholesale Food Company has just had a Frame Relay circuit installed to its local central office (CO) by the telco carrier. The network administrator must confirm that the router and Frame Relay switch are able to communicate successfully.

Cable a network that is similar to the one in Figure 15-1.1. You can use any router that meets the interface requirements in Figure 15-1.1 (that is, 800, 1600, 1700, 2500, and 2600 routers or a combination). Refer to the information in Appendix C, "Router Interface Summary Chart," to correctly specify the interface identifiers based on the equipment in your lab. The 1721 series routers produced the configuration output in this lab. Another router might produce slightly different output. You should execute the following steps on each router unless you are specifically instructed otherwise. Start a HyperTerminal session.

Implement the procedure documented in Appendix A, "Erasing and Reloading the Router," on all routers before you continue with this lab.

Step 1. Configure the routers.

Configure the host name, console, VTY, and enable passwords according to Table 15-1.1. If you have difficulty doing this, refer to Lab 11-1, "Configuring NAT (TI 1.1.4a)."

Step 2. Configure the serial interface.

A.   In Frame Relay, the customer router is considered to be the DTE device. To configure the serial interface, you must define the Layer 2 Frame Relay frame type. To configure the frame type, use the following commands:

```
Cork#configure terminal
Cork(config)#interface serial 0
Cork(config-if)#encapsulation frame-relay IETF
```

B.   Next, you need to configure the format of the Frame Relay management protocol. To configure the Local Management Interface (LMI) type, use the following commands:

```
Cork(config-if)#frame-relay lmi-type ansi
Cork(config-if)#no shutdown
Cork(config-if)#ctrl+z
```

Step 3. Verify the Frame Relay configuration

A.   To verify the configuration, use the show interface commands that are related to Frame Relay. To view the serial interface configuration, enter the following command:

```
Cork#show interface serial 0
```

B.   What is the state of the interface? Serial 0 is _____ line protocol is _____

C.   What is the encapsulation type? _____

D.   What state is the DTE LMI in? _____

E.   What is the LMI type? _____

Step 4. Review switch assignments.

A.   To verify that the DLCIs are defined on the switch, use **show frame-relay pvc**.
       The DLCIs are learned by the router via LMI and can be viewed.

```
Cork#show frame-relay pvc
```

B.   What DLCI numbers are available on the switch? _____

C.   What is the PVC status of the first DLCI? _____

Step 5. Check the Frame Relay map.

```
Cork#show frame-relay map
```

The output from this command shows that none of the DLCIs, defined on the switch, are
in use. The PVC is inactive and there is no current mapping between the Layer 2 DLCI
and Layer 3 IP address, as shown in the **show frame-relay map** command output.

After you complete the previous steps, log off (by typing **exit**) and turn the router off. Then
remove and store the cables and adapter.

Lab 15-2   Configuring Frame Relay PVC (TI 5.2.2)

Figure 15-2.1   Topology for Lab 15-2

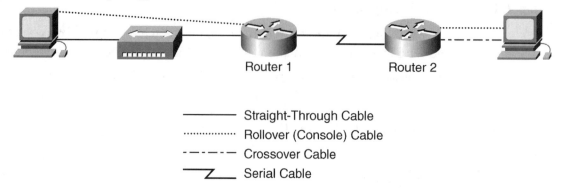

Router 1   Router 2

```
————————     Straight-Through Cable
··············     Rollover (Console) Cable
— — — —     Crossover Cable
———Z———     Serial Cable
```

Table 15-2.1 Lab Equipment Configuration

Router Designation	Router Name	Interface Type	Serial 0 Address/Subnet Mask	Fast Ethernet 0 Address/ Subnet Mask	DLCI Number
Router 1	Washington	DCE	192.168.1.1/24	192.168.3.1/24	102
Router 2	Dublin	DTE	192.168.1.2/24	192.168.2.1/24	102

The enable secret password for both routers is **class**.

The enable, VTY, and console password for both routers is **cisco**.

Objective

Configure two routers back to back as a Frame Relay PVC. You will do this manually, in the absence of a frame relay switch, and therefore there will be no Local Management Interface (LMI).

Background/Preparation

Cable a network that is similar to the one in Figure 15-2.1. You can use any router that meets the interface requirements in Figure 15-2.1 (that is, 800, 1600, 1700, 2500, and 2600 routers or a combination). Refer to the information in Appendix C to correctly specify the interface identifiers based on the equipment in your lab. The 1721 series routers produced the configuration output in this lab. Another router might produce slightly different output. You should execute the following steps on each router unless you are specifically instructed otherwise. Start a HyperTerminal session.

Implement the procedure documented in Appendix A on all routers before you continue with this lab.

Step 1. Configure the routers.

Configure the host name, console, VTY, and enable passwords according to Table 15-2.1. If you have difficulty doing this, refer to Lab 11-1, "Configuring NAT (TI 1.1.4a)."

Step 2. Configure the Washington serial interface

First, define the Frame Relay frame type to be used on this link. To configure the encapsulation type, use the command **encapsulation frame-relay ietf**. Disable keepalive messages because there is no Frame Relay switch in this configuration (and consequently no Frame Relay DCE).

```
Washington#configure terminal
Washington(config-if)#interface serial 0
Washington(config-if)#encapsulation frame-relay ietf
Washington(config-if)#no keepalive
Washington(config-if)#ip address 192.168.1.1 255.255.255.0
Washington(config-if)#no shutdown
```

Step 3. Configure the Frame Relay map on Washington.

A. When you are sending an Ethernet frame to a remote IP address, you must discover the remote MAC address so that you can construct the correct frame type. Frame relay needs a similar mapping.

B. The remote IP address needs to be mapped to the local DLCI (Layer 2 address), so the correctly addressed frame can be created locally for this PVC. Because you cannot map the DLCI automatically, with LMI disabled, you must create this map manually by using the frame-relay map command. The *broadcast* parameter allows IP broadcasts to use the same mapping for crossing this PVC.

```
Washington(config-if)#frame-relay map ip 192.168.1.2 102 ietf
broadcast
```

Step 4. Configure the DCE on Washington.

In this configuration using DCE cables, a clock signal is necessary. The bandwidth command is optional, but it is a wise choice for verifying bandwidth transmission. Another option is to title the connection by using the description command. This is useful so that you can record information about the PVC, such as a remote contact person and the leased line circuit identifier.

```
Washington(config-if)#clockrate 64000
Washington(config-if)#bandwidth 64
Washington(config-if)#description PVC to Dublin, DLCI 102, Circuit
#DASS465875,
 Contact John Tobin (061-8886745)
```

Step 5. Configure the Dublin router.

Configure the Dublin router by using the following commands:

```
Dublin#configure terminal
Dublin(config-if)#interface serial 0
Dublin(config-if)#encapsulation frame-relay ietf
Dublin(config-if)#no keepalive
Dublin(config-if)#no shutdown
Dublin(config-if)#ip address 192.168.1.2 255.255.255.0
Dublin(config-if)#frame-relay map ip 192.168.1.1 102 ietf broadcast
```

```
Dublin(config-if)#bandwidth 64
Dublin(config-if)#description PVC to Washington, DLCI 102, Circuit
#DASS465866
  Contact Pat White (091-6543211)
```

Step 6. Verify the Frame Relay PVC.

    A.   On the Washington router, type the command **show frame-relay pvc**:

```
Washington#show frame-relay pvc
```

    B.   What is the DLCI number that is reported? _____

    C.   What is the PVC status? _____

    D.   What is the value of the DLCI USAGE? _____

Step 7. Display the Frame Relay map.

    A.   To view the Layer 2 to Layer 3 mapping, use the **show frame-relay map** command at the privileged EXEC mode prompt:

```
Washington#show frame-relay map
```

    B.   What is the IP address shown? _____

    C.   In what state is interface serial 0? _____

Step 8. Verify Frame Relay connectivity.

    A.   From the Washington router, **ping** the Dublin router serial interface.

    B.   Was the **ping** successful? _____

    C.   If not, troubleshoot router configurations.

After you complete the previous steps, log off (by typing **exit**) and turn the router off. Then remove and store the cables and adapter.

Lab 15-3   Configuring Frame Relay Subinterfaces (TI 5.2.5)

Figure 15-3.1   Topology for Lab 15-3

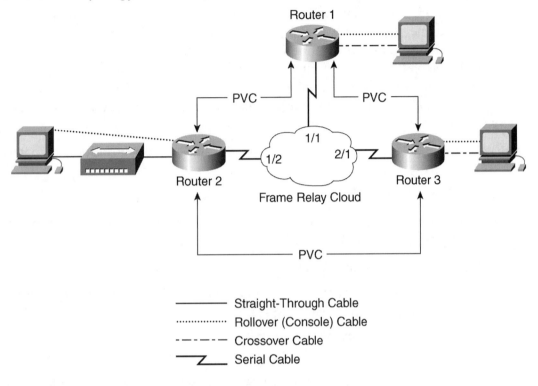

Table 15-3.1 Lab Equipment Configuration

Router Designation	Router Name	Interface Type	Serial 0 Address/ Subnet Mask	DLCI Number	Fast Ethernet 0 Address/ Subnet Mask
Router 1	Amsterdam	DTE	192.168.4.1/24	102	192.168.1.1/24
			192.168.5.1/24	103	
Router 2	Paris	DTE	192.168.4.2/24	201	192.168.2.1/24
			192.168.6.1/24	203	
Router 3	Berlin	DTE	192.168.5.2/24	301	192.168.3.1/24
			192.168.6.2/24	302	

The enable secret password for all routers is **class**.

The enable, VTY, and console password for all routers is **cisco**.

The routing protocol for all routers is IGRP 100.

Objective

Configure three routers in a full-mesh Frame Relay network.

Background/Preparation

This lab uses an Adtran Atlas550 Frame Relay to simulate the switch/Frame Relay cloud.

Cable a network that is similar to the one in Figure 15-3.1. You can use any router that meets the interface requirements in Figure 15-3.1 (that is, 800, 1600, 1700, 2500, and 2600 routers or a combination). Refer to the information in Appendix C to correctly specify the interface identifiers based on the equipment in your lab. The 1721 series routers produced the configuration output in this lab. Another router might produce slightly different output. You should execute the following steps on each router unless you are specifically instructed otherwise. Start a HyperTerminal session.

Implement the procedure documented in Appendix A on all routers before you continue with this lab.

Step 1. Configure the routers.

Configure the host name, console, VTY, and enable passwords according to Table 15-3.1. If you have difficulty doing this, refer to Lab 11-1, "Configuring NAT (TI 1.1.4a)."

Step 2. Configure the Serial 0 interfaces.

A. First, you must define the Frame Relay encapsulation type to be used on this link by using the following commands:

```
Amsterdam#configure terminal
Amsterdam(config)#interface serial 0
Amsterdam(config-if)#encapsulation frame-relay ietf
Amsterdam(config-if)#frame-relay lmi-type ansi
```

B. Use a description field to store relevant information, such as the circuit number, if you have to report a line fault.

```
Amsterdam(config-if)#description Circuit #KPN465555
Amsterdam(config-if)#no shutdown
```

C. The same commands are used to configure the Berlin and Paris routers.

```
Paris(config)#interface serial 0
Paris(config-if)#encapsulation frame-relay ietf
Paris(config-if)#frame-relay lmi-type ansi
Paris(config-if)#description Circuit #FRT372826
Paris(config-if)#no shutdown

Berlin(config)#interface serial 0
Berlin(config-if)#encapsulation frame-relay ietf
```

```
Berlin(config-if)#frame-relay lmi-type ansi

Berlin(config-if)#description Circuit #DTK465866

Berlin(config-if)#no shutdown
```

Step 3. Create subinterfaces on the Amsterdam router.

For each of the PVCs, create a subinterface on the serial port. This subinterface will be a point-to-point configuration. For consistency and future troubleshooting, use the DLCI number as the subinterface number. The commands to create a subinterface are as follows:

```
Amsterdam(config-if)#interface serial 0.102 point-to-point

Amsterdam(config-if)#description PVC to Paris, DLCI 102, Contact Rick
Voight(+33-1-5534-2234) Circuit #FRT372826

Amsterdam(config-if)#ip address 192.168.4.1 255.255.255.0

Amsterdam(config-if)#frame-relay interface-dlci 102

Amsterdam(config-if)#interface serial 0.103 point-to-point

Amsterdam(config-if)#description PVC to Berlin, DLCI 103, Contact P
Wills(+49- 61 03 / 7 65 72 00) Circuit #DTK465866

Amsterdam(config-if)#ip address 192.168.5.1 255.255.255.0

Amsterdam(config-if)#frame-relay interface-dlci 103
```

Step 4. Create subinterfaces on the Paris router.

To configure the subinterfaces on the Paris router, use the following commands:

```
Paris(config-if)#interface Serial 0.201 point-to-point

Paris(config-if)#description PVC to Amsterdam, DLCI 201, Contact Peter
Muller (+31 20 623 32 67) Circuit #KPN465555

Paris(config-if)#ip address 192.168.4.2 255.255.255.0

Paris(config-if)#frame-relay interface-dlci 201

Paris(config-if)#interface Serial 0.203 point-to-point

Paris(config-if)#description PVC to Berlin, DLCI 203, Contact Peter
Willis (+49- 61 03 / 7 66 72 00) Circuit #DTK465866

Paris(config-if)#ip address 192.168.6.1 255.255.255.0

Paris(config-if)#frame-relay interface-dlci 203
```

Step 5. Create subinterfaces on the Berlin router.

To configure the subinterfaces on the Berlin router, use the following commands:

```
Berlin(config-if)#interface Serial 0.301 point-to-point

Berlin(config-if)#description PVC to Amsterdam, DLCI 301, Contact Peter
Muller (+31 20 623 32 67) Circuit #KPN465555

Berlin(config-if)#ip address 192.168.5.2 255.255.255.0

Berlin(config-if)#frame-relay interface-dlci 301

Berlin(config-if)#interface Serial 0.302 point-to-point
```

```
Berlin(config-if)#description PVC to Paris, DLCI 302, Contact Rick
Voight (+33-1-5534-2234) Circuit #FRT372826

Berlin(config-if)#ip address 192.168.6.2 255.255.255.0

Berlin(config-if)#frame-relay interface-dlci 302
```

Step 6. Configure IGRP routing.

To configure the routing protocol IGRP 100, use the following configuration:

```
Amsterdam(config-if)#router igrp 100

Amsterdam(config-router)#network 192.168.1.0

Amsterdam(config-router)#network 192.168.4.0

Amsterdam(config-router)#network 192.168.5.0


Paris(config-if)#router igrp 100
Paris(config-router)#network 192.168.2.0
Paris(config-router)#network 192.168.4.0
Paris(config-router)#network 192.168.6.0


Berlin(config-if)#router igrp 100
Berlin(config-router)#network 192.168.3.0
Berlin(config-router)#network 192.168.5.0
Berlin(config-router)#network 192.168.6.0
```

Step 7. Verify the Frame Relay PVC.

A.   On the Amsterdam router, issue the command show frame-relay pvc:

```
Amsterdam#show frame-relay pvc
```

B.   How many active local PVCs exist? _____

C.   What is the interface value? _____

D.   What is the PVC status? _____

E.   Which DLCI number is inactive? _____

F.   From this, you can see that three DLCIs are defined on this Frame Relay circuit, and only two of them are in use. This is the way the Adtran 550 emulator has been configured. It is useful output because it shows what you would see if a DLCI were defined on the Frame Relay switch but not configured on the router. The other DLCIs, 102 and 103, are ACTIVE and are associated with their respective subinterfaces. It also shows that some packets have passed across the PVC.

Step 8. Show the Frame Relay maps.

A.   Look at the Frame Relay maps by typing the command **show frame-relay map** at the privileged EXEC mode prompt:

```
Amsterdam#show frame-relay map
```

B.   What is the status of the links? _____

C.   What type are the DLCIs defined as? _____

D.   Are the DLCIs the same on the Paris router? _____

Step 9. Show the LMIs.

A.   Look at the LMI statistics by using the **show frame-relay lmi** command:

```
Amsterdam#show frame-relay lmi
```

B.   Which fields have non-zero counter values? _____

C.   What is the LMI type? _____

Step 10. Check the routing protocol.

A.   Use the **show ip route** command to verify that the PVCs are up and active:

```
Amsterdam#show ip route
```

B.   Is the routing protocol working? _____

C.   If not, troubleshoot the router configurations.

D.   List the IGRP routes._____ _____

_____

Step 11. Verify connectivity.

A.   **Ping** the Fast Ethernet interfaces.

B.   Were the **ping**s successful? _____

C.   If not, troubleshoot the router configurations and repeat this step.

After you complete the previous steps, log off (by typing **exit**) and turn the router off. Then remove and store the cables and adapter.

Lab 15-4 Configuring a Router as a Frame Relay Switch

Figure 15-4.1 Topology for Lab 15-4

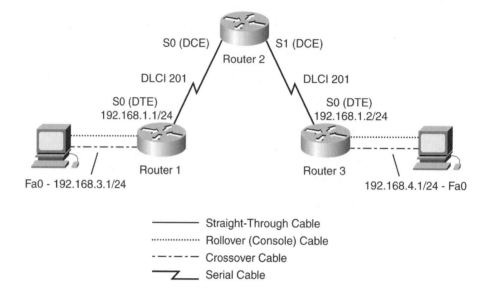

Table 15-4.1 Lab Equipment Configuration I

Router Designation	Router Name	Serial 0 Address/ Subnet Mask	Interface Type	DLCI Number	Fast Ethernet 0 Address/ Subnet Mask
Router 1	Site1	192.168.1.1/24	DTE	102	192.168.3.1/24
Router 2 (switch)	FRSwitch	No IP Address	DCE	102	Not used
Router 3	Site2	192.168.1.2/24	DTE	201	192.168.4.1/24

Table 15-4.2 Lab Equipment Configuration II

Router Designation	Router Name	Serial 1 Address/ Subnet Mask	Interface Type	DLCI Number	Network Statements
Router 1	Site1	Not used	N/A	N/A	192.168.1.0 192.168.3.0
Router 2 (switch)	FRSwitch	No IP Address	DCE	201	None
Router 3	Site2	Not used	N/A	N/A	192.168.1.0 192.168.4.0

The enable secret password for all routers is **class**.

The enable, VTY, and console password for all routers is **cisco**.

The routing protocol for all routers is IGRP 100.

Objectives

- Use a router to emulate a Frame Relay switch between two WAN links

- Configure a router to act as a Frame Relay switch with DCE on both serial interfaces

- Configure two routers as DTE devices to communicate through the Frame Relay switch

Background/Preparation

Cable a network that is similar to the one in Figure 15-3.1. You can use any router that meets the interface requirements in Figure 15-3.1 (that is, 800, 1600, 1700, 2500, and 2600 routers or a combination). Refer to the information in Appendix C to correctly specify the interface identifiers based on the equipment in your lab. The 1721 series routers produced the configuration output in this lab. Another router might produce slightly different output. You should execute the following steps on each router unless you are specifically instructed otherwise.

The two cables connected to the middle router (Router 2) should both be DCE in order to have this router emulate the Frame Relay switch (DCE and DTE cables are labeled on one end). On Router 2, connect one of the DCE cables to Serial 0 and the other to Serial 1. The DCE cable from Router 2 serial 0 will connect to a DTE cable going to Router 1 serial 0 and the Router 2 serial 1 cable will go to the Router 3 DTE cable on serial 0. Start a HyperTerminal session.

Implement the procedure documented in Appendix A on all routers before you continue with this lab.

Step 1. Configure the routers.

    A.   Configure the 3 routers according to Tables 15-4.1 and 15-4.2. If you have difficulty doing this, refer to Lab 11-1, "Configuring NAT (TI 1.1.4a)."

    B.   Use the **show controller** command to check the DCE/DTE connections for each router serial interface being used.

```
Site1#show controller serial 0
```

    C.   What does the **show controller** command for Serial 0 indicate? _____

Step 2. Check the status of the Serial 0 WAN interface on the Site1 router.

    A.   Use **show interface** command

```
Site1# show interface serial 0
```

    B.   What is the IP address and number of subnet bits for this interface? _____

C.   What is the status of the interface and the Line protocol? _____

D.   What is the encapsulation currently set to? _____

Step 3. Configure the Serial 0 interface on Site1 for a Frame Relay connection.

A.   Use the following commands to set up Frame Relay on interface Serial 0. Note that if you are using Cisco IOS Release 11.2 or later the Frame Relay DLCI and LMI type can be detected automatically and will not need to be configured manually.

```
Site1#config t

Site1(config)# interface serial 0

Site1(config-if)# encapsulation frame-relay

Site1(config-if)# no shutdown
```

B.   Verify the configuration of interface serial 0.

```
Site1#show interface serial 0
```

Step 4. Check the status of the Serial 0 WAN interface on the Site2 router.

A.   Use the **show interface** command

```
Site2# show interface serial 0
```

B.   What is the IP address and number of subnet bits for this interface?

_____

C.   What is the status of the interface and the Line protocol? _____

D.   What is the encapsulation currently set to? _____

Step 5. Configure the Serial 0 interface on Site2 for a Frame Relay connection.

A.   Use the following commands to set up Frame Relay on interface Serial 1. Note that if you are using Cisco IOS version 11.2 or later the Frame Relay DLCI and LMI type can be detected automatically.

```
Site2#config t
Site2(config)# interface Serial 0
Site2(config-if)# encapsulation frame-relay
Site2(config-if)# no shutdown
```

B.   Verify the configuration of interface serial 0.

```
Site2#sh int s0
```

Step 6. Configure the FRSwitch router as a Frame Relay switch.

Use the following commands to enable Frame Relay switching and define interfaces Serial 0 and Serial 1 as DCE.

```
FRSwitch#config t
FRSwitch(config)# frame-relay switching
FRSwitch(config)# interface Serial 0
FRSwitch(config-if)# no ip address
FRSwitch(config-if)# encapsulation frame-relay
FRSwitch(config-if)# clock rate 56000
```

```
FRSwitch(config-if)# frame-relay intf-type dce
FRSwitch(config-if)# frame-relay route 201 interface serial 1 102
FRSwitch(config-if)# no shutdown

FRSwitch(config)# interface Serial 1
FRSwitch(config-if)# no ip address
FRSwitch(config-if)# encapsulation frame-relay
FRSwitch(config-if)# clock rate 56000
FRSwitch(config-if)# frame-relay intf-type dce
FRSwitch(config-if)# frame-relay route 102 interface serial 0 201
FRSwitch(config-if)# no shutdown
```

Step 7. Verify the configuration of interfaces serial 0 and serial 1 using the **show running-config** command.

```
FRSwitch#sh run
```

A.   What information was displayed about FRSwitch interface S0?

_____

_____

B.   What information was displayed about FRSwitch interface S1?

_____

_____

Step 8. Confirm that the Frame Relay link is up on Site1 by entering the **show interface serial 0** command.

```
Site1# sh int s0
```

A.   What is the status of the serial frame link? _____

B.   How many LMI messages were sent and received? _____

C.   What does this mean? _____

D.   What is the LMI type? _____

Step 9. Verify the Frame Relay PVC status for Site1.

```
Site1# show frame pvc
```

A.   What is the DLCI number of the connection? _____

B.   What is the status of the PVC? _____

Step 10. Check the Frame Relay map for Site1.

```
Site1# show frame-relay map
```

A.   What is local interface number, IP address of the switch interface and the DLCI of the connection? _____

B.   What is the status of the PVC? _____

Step 11. Check the LMI status for Site1.

```
Site1# show frame-relay lmi
```

What is local interface number and is it DCE or DTE? _____

Step 12. Verify the Frame Relay PVC status for FRSwitch.

> FRSwitch# **show frame-relay pvc**

    A.   What are the DLCI numbers of the connections? _____

    B.   What is the status of the PVCs? _____

Step 13. Verify the Frame Relay routing table for FRSwitch.

> FRSwitch# **show frame-relay route**

What information is shown? _____

Step 14. Verify connectivity from Site1 to Site2 through the switch.

    A.   **Ping** the Fast Ethernet interfaces.

    B.   Were the **ping**s successful? _____

    C.   If not, troubleshoot the router configurations and repeat this step.

After you complete the previous steps, log off (by typing **exit**) and turn the router off. Then remove and store the cables and adapter.

CCNA 4

Chapter 16: Introduction to Network Administration

There are no hands-on labs associated with the topic of this chapter. Please review the information in Chapter 16 of the *Cisco Networking Academy Program CCNA 3 and 4 Companion Guide* to ensure that you can do the following:

- Explain important aspects of Windows, UNIX, and Linux workstations
- Explain the functions of network servers
- Understand network operating systems (NOSs)

CCNA 4

Chapter 17: Optical Networking Fundamentals

There are no hands-on labs associated with the topic of this chapter. Please review the information in Chapter 17 of the *Cisco Networking Academy Program CCNA 3 and 4 Companion Guide* to ensure that you can do the following:

- Identify the key business drivers of optical networks
- Describe the features of fiber-optic systems
- Describe the communication components in an optical communication system
- Identify the wavelength of the light used in optical transmission
- Identify the features of the light-emitting devices used in optical transmission
- Describe important design characteristics of fiber and the index of refraction (IOR)
- Identify the main components of a fiber-optic cable
- Describe the features of multimode fiber
- Describe the features of single-mode fiber
- Explain the possible fiber geometry problems
- Describe different loss factors in fiber, including connector loss, macrobending, microbending, and absorption
- Identify the causes of attenuation in optical fiber
- Identify the effects of different types of dispersion
- Describe how to obtain the greatest capacity from optical fiber
- Describe the optical filter technology and identify the functions of the optical amplifier
- Describe how erbium-doped fiber amplifiers (EDFAs) work
- Describe Synchronous Optical Network (SONET) technology
- Describe SONET/Synchronous Digital Hierarchy (SDH)
- Describe what dense wavelength division multiplexing (DWDM) systems are
- Explain how electrical/optical/electrical (E/O/E) conversion (transponder) works
- Describe fiber-optic data transmission
- Describe the advantages of DWDM
- Describe the features of metropolitan DWDM

Part III   Appendixes

Appendix A: Erasing and Reloading the Router

Appendix B: Erasing and Reloading the Switch

Appendix C: Router Interface and Summary Chart

Appendix A

Erasing and Reloading the Router

For the majority of the labs in CCNA 3 and CCNA 4 focusing on router configuration, it is necessary to start with a basic unconfigured router; otherwise, the configuration parameters you enter might combine with previous ones and produce unpredictable results. The instructions here allow you to prepare the router prior to performing the lab so that previous configuration options do not interfere with your configurations.

The following is the procedure for clearing out previous configurations and starting with an unconfigured router. The prompts and responses may vary somewhat depending on the router model and IOS version but the basic procedure will be the same.

1. Enter into privileged EXEC mode by typing **enable**.

   ```
   Router> enable
   ```

   If prompted for a password, enter **class**. (If that does not work, ask your instructor.)

2. In privileged EXEC mode, enter the command **erase startup-config**:

   ```
   Router# erase startup-config
   ```

   The responding line prompt will be

   ```
   Erasing the nvram filesystem will remove all files! Continue?
   [confirm]
   ```

3. Press **Enter** to confirm.

   The response will be

   ```
   Erase of nvram: complete
   ```

4. Now in privileged EXEC mode, enter the command **reload**:

   ```
   Router(config)# reload
   ```

   If the responding line prompt is

   ```
   System configuration has been modified. Save? [yes/no]:
   ```

5. Type **n** and then **Enter**.

   The responding line prompt will be

   ```
   Proceed with reload? [confirm]
   ```

6. Press **Enter** to confirm.

   In the first line of the response will be

   ```
   Reload requested by console.
   ```

After the router reloads, the line prompt will be

```
Would you like to enter the initial configuration dialog?
[yes/no]:
```

7.   Type **n** and then **Enter**.

If the responding line prompt is

Would you like to terminate autoinstall? [yes]:

8.   Press **Enter** to confirm.

```
The responding line prompt will be
```

```
Press RETURN to get started!
```

9.   Press **Enter**.

Now the router is ready for you to perform the assigned lab.

Appendix B

Erasing and Reloading the Switch

For the majority of the labs in CCNA 3 and CCNA 4 focusing on switch configuration, it is necessary to start with a basic unconfigured switch; otherwise, the configuration parameters you enter might combine with previous ones and produce unpredictable results. The instructions here allow you to prepare the switch prior to performing the lab so that previous configuration options do not interfere with your configurations.

The following is the procedure for clearing out previous configurations and starting with an unconfigured switch. Instructions are provided for the 2900, 2950, and 1900 Series switches. The prompts and responses may vary somewhat depending on the switch model and IOS version but the basic procedure will be the same.

2900 and 2950 Series Switches

Step 1. Disconnect all data cables from all switch ports. This is a critical step since information from one switch can automatically propagate to another if there is a cable between them.

Step 2. Enter into the privileged EXEC mode by typing **enable**.

If prompted for a password, enter **class** (if that does not work, ask the instructor).

```
Switch> enable
```

Step 3. Remove the VLAN database information file.

```
Switch# delete flash:vlan.dat
Delete filename [vlan.dat]? [Enter]
Delete flash:vlan.dat? [confirm] [Enter]
```

If there was no VLAN file, this following message appears:

```
%Error deleting flash:vlan.dat (No such file or directory)
```

Step 4. Remove the switch startup configuration file from NVRAM.

```
Switch# erase startup-config
```

The responding line prompt will be

```
Erasing the nvram filesystem will remove all files! Continue?
[confirm]
```

Press **Enter** to confirm

The response should be

```
Erase of nvram: complete
```

Step 5. Software restart using the **reload** command.

    A.   At the privileged EXEC mode enter the command **reload**.

```
Switch(config)# reload
```

If the responding line prompt is

```
System configuration has been modified. Save? [yes/no]:
```

    B.   Type **n** and then press **Enter**.

The responding line prompt will be

```
Proceed with reload? [confirm] [Enter]
```

The first line of the response will be

```
Reload requested by console.
```

After the switch has reloaded, the line prompt will be

```
Would you like to enter the initial configuration dialog?
[yes/no]:
```

    C.   Type **n** and then press **Enter**.

The responding line prompt will be

```
Press RETURN to get started! [Enter]
```

1900 Series Switches

Step 1. Disconnect all data cables from all switch ports. This is a critical step since information from one switch can automatically propagate to another if there is a cable between them.

Step 2. Remove VLAN Trunking Protocol (VTP) information.

```
#delete vtp
This command resets the switch with VTP parameters set to factory
     defaults.
All other parameters will be unchanged.

Reset system with VTP parameters set to factory defaults, [Y]es or
[N]o?
```

Enter **y** and press **Enter**.

Step 3. Remove the switch startup configuration from NVRAM.

```
#delete nvram
This command resets the switch with factory defaults.  All system
parameters will revert to their default factory settings.  All
static and dynamic addresses will be removed.

Reset system with factory defaults, [Y]es or [N]o?
```

Enter **y** and press [**Enter**.

Appendix C

Router Interface Summary Chart

For most of the CCNA 3 and 4 labs, you need to examine the following chart to correctly reference the router interface identifiers to use in commands based on the equipment in your lab.

Note: If you have console or telnet access to the router, use the command **show ip interface brief** to see a list of interfaces and their proper designations. You may also look at the physical interfaces to identify what type and how many interfaces the router has.

Router Model	Ethernet Interface #1	Ethernet Interface #2	Serial Interface #1	Serial Interface #2
800 (806)	Ethernet 0 (E0)	Ethernet 1 (E1)		
1600	Ethernet 0 (E0)	Ethernet 1 (E1)	Serial 0 (S0)	Serial 1 (S1)
1700	FastEthernet 0 (FA0)	FastEthernet 1 (FA1)	Serial 0 (S0)	Serial 1 (S1)
2500	Ethernet 0 (E0)	Ethernet 1 (E1)	Serial 0 (S0)	Serial 1 (S1)
2600	FastEthernet 0/0 (FA0/0)	FastEthernet 0/1 (FA0/1)	Serial 0/0 (S0/0)	Serial 0/1 (S0/1)

There is no way to effectively list all of the combinations of configurations for each router class. The chart provides the identifiers for the possible combinations of interfaces in the device. This interface chart does not include any other type of interface even though a specific router might contain one. An example of this is an ISDN BRI interface. The string in parentheses is the legal abbreviation that you can use in Cisco IOS Software commands to represent the interface.

NOTES

NOTES

NOTES

NOTES

NOTES

NOTES

NOTES

NOTES

NOTES

NOTES

NOTES